Brother Shen,
leader of China Gospel
Fellowship, one of China's
foremost house church
movements.

NO LIMITATIONS

Brother Shen Xiao Feng – his story and writings
with Dr. David Hunt

WorldServe Publishing Inc.

"Pastor Shen Xiao Feng's book provides an intimate conversation on the backgrounds and current state of the Church in China. It is truly a primer on basic Christianity, a badly needed gift to the American church."

Michael Card, Author, Teacher, Songwriter.

"Such a book is rarely written. It takes courage. It involves risk. Yet the man is willing to tell his story. His writing reveals much that is unknown. It describes the complexities facing the Chinese Church. No one reading this book can remain uninspired."

Tetsunao Yamamori, International Director, LCWE

NO LIMITATIONS
By Brother Shen Xiao Feng

Published by WorldServe Publishing
Cover Design: Idou Design
Printed in Canada by Transcontinental Printing Inc, 2006

ISBN 1 894685 52-0

Unless otherwise noted, Scripture quotations are from the New International Version of the Bible.

CONTENTS

The first family photo

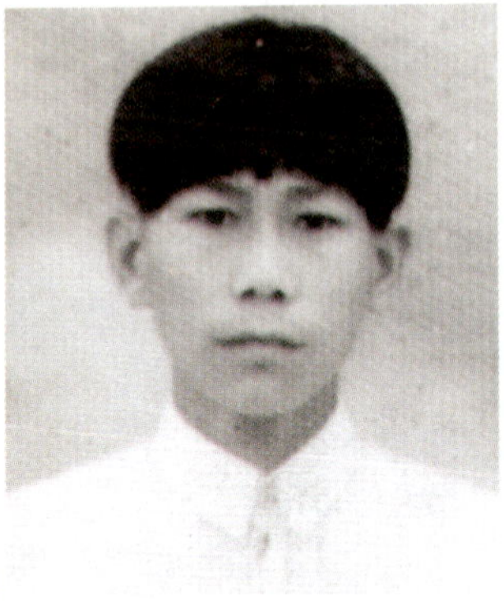

An angry young man before Christ.

A gift from above. Brother Shen's precious wife who has stood with him, run with him, prayed with him, laughed with him, cried with him and bravely continues to stand by his side as together they serve the house church in China.

Brother Shen today, continuing to bravely and faithfully serve the Lord as the head of China Gospel Fellowship

Brother Shen's first covert in prison, he serving time for preaching the Gospel, the other man a common criminal but now a brother in Christ.

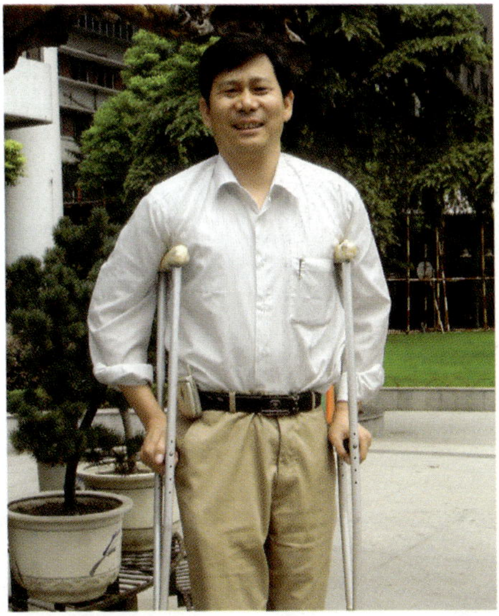

PRECIOUS PHOTOS FROM A LIFETIME

Roughly one picture per decade of his life is all Brother Shen has left in his possession. Over the years, all the rest of the photos from his life have been confiscated and destroyed.

Brother Shen thought long and hard about whether he should share this precious treasure with all of us but after much prayer and thought, he and his family and the leadership of China Gospel Fellowship decided to share these personal photos with the Christian public, worldwide.

Please remember to pray for Brother Shen, his family, his ministry and for God's faithful, suffering servants in China. Please pray for God's protection, blessing and provision for them.

FOREWORD

by Dr. David Hunt
President, WorldServe Ministries

No Limitations will give you a rare glimpse into the Underground Church in China through the eyes of one of its foremost leaders, Brother Shen Xiao Feng, leader of China Gospel Fellowship with 10 million believers.

The telling of this story—never before shared with the outside world—is remarkable for many reasons. It is unusual in that a current leader of one of China's largest house church movements has felt led to publicly share his story while still actively ministering and under the threat of arrest.

It is also unusual in that Brother Shen is very candid about his struggles and very honest in his assessment of some of the challenges facing the house church movements of China in the 21st Century.

I have been privileged to spend much time with this precious brother, but years ago, prior to meeting him, I only knew him by reputation. The day I met him, I was surprised to see his physical handicap—crutches to support legs crippled by disease since childhood. I thought surely this must have placed a great limitation on him and his ministry and leadership.

When I heard Brother Shen share of his early years, the malnutrition, the sicknesses, the hardships, I thought of how they too must have limited him in many ways. However, as I spent more time with this precious brother, I learned that these many hardships and challenges have resulted in the opposite. Instead of limiting him, God has used these handicaps and hardships to forge Brother Shen into the very strong person he is today, equipped ideally for the Kingdom's work.

I came to the conclusion that he has *no limitations.*

From man's perspective, he would be one of the least likely candidates for his very high level of responsibility. From God's perspective, he was a weak enough vessel that God in His power could work through him with unrestrained might.

I have had the great privilege to know and work with some of God's choice servants in the world today—many of them molded by suffering and extreme circumstances into church planting movement leaders. Interestingly, they all have this one thing in common: they are weak enough and frail enough to allow God to work through them with His great power and accomplish His work through them with *no limitations*.

I often refer to 2 Corinthians 4 as a passage that explains this wonderful, upside-down Kingdom of God being lived out in the lives of His special servants:

> *But we have this treasure in jars of clay to show that this all-surpassing power is from God and not from us. We are hard pressed on every side, but not crushed; perplexed, but not in despair; persecuted, but not abandoned; struck down, but not destroyed. We always carry around in our body the death of Jesus, so that the life of Jesus may also be revealed in our body. For we who are alive are always being given over to death for Jesus' sake, so that his life may be revealed in our mortal body. So then, death is at work in us, but life is at work in you.*
>
> ***2 Corinthians 4:7-12***

Brother Shen could only have accomplished what he has by carrying around the death of Jesus in his body so that Christ's supernatural life would be revealed. Out of great weakness, in the face of great persecution, as this weak vessel, God has worked with *no limitations*.

Dear friend, I would ask that before you read this story and some of the writings of Brother Shen, ask the Lord to open your eyes to see what He would have you see. God is not limited by our weakness, human frailties, lack of education, our age—either too young or too old. Whatever our preconceptions may be, that does not limit our Sovereign, Mighty God. We limit Him by our strength, our ability, our education, our wealth, our lack of vision and obedience.

The Lord doesn't need your strength. He needs your weakness, your dependence upon Him. He needs a vessel through which He can work with relentless power and "show that this all-surpassing power is from God." That doesn't mean He won't use your abilities and areas where you are strong, but when we stop relying on those things and rely on the dynamic of the Spirit of God, then He can also work through us with *no limitations*.

The Underground Church in China is the spotless Bride of Christ—perfect and pure, not because it doesn't have any faults, but because it has been washed by the blood of the Lamb.

May we not look at what is wrong with the Church; rather, may we be inspired by their faith, their sacrifice, their walk with the Savior and the fruit of their lives and ministry. It is time we change our perspective and see it for what it is—one of the most dynamic churches in Christian history, anointed and used of God.

My prayer for you as you read this book is that you would come to the place Brother Shen did and surrender all—your weaknesses and your strengths—becoming that vessel God can work through.

Beyond that, my prayer is that you would better understand the Underground Church in China that is so misrepresented by so many.

As you gain understanding, may the Lord move you to join with us and with the underground house church movements in China to bring them desperately needed encouragement and financial help. You can make a difference in the lives and ministries of God's choice servants in the house church movements in China. It is our responsibility—it is our high honor.

May our loving and gracious Heavenly Father begin a fresh work in your life today!

PREFACE

by Brother Shen Xiao Feng

Because of certain "abnormal" circumstances recently, it was not possible for me to travel around for ministry, so I was forced to stay at home and wait upon the Lord. Amidst the silence and solitude of inactivity, many memories of the past flashed before my eyes. I pondered the years from my birth to my experience of God's saving grace, to my twenty years of forced exile from my hometown; the guiding hand of God was there every step of the way. His care and protection was evident throughout, and despite undergoing a baptism of fire, I now find myself in a land of abundance.

In reviewing the 20-year history of the Chinese house churches, I see many brothers and sisters in Christ who, out of their love for the Lord, dedicated their lives for the sake of the Gospel. They devoted their blood, sweat and tears to bringing the good news to every nook and cranny of our beloved motherland. They sowed the seeds of the Gospel that produced the present harvest of souls for which we can celebrate and rejoice. They willingly gave of their youthful vitality and strength in faithful service and obedience to the Lord's gospel mandate. It was a journey marked by humiliation, poverty and hard work, but "those who sow in tears will reap with songs of joy." Psalm 126:6

As we enter into the 21st Century, we in the Chinese Church need to seriously reflect upon the road already traveled and the enormous challenges that lie before us. How are we to handle the ever-increasing openness in Chinese politics and the impact of secularism upon family morals and values? To these questions and more, this servant of God shares his shallow insights with other beloved members of the Body of Christ. My hope is that my humble contributions will bring forth treasures from the storehouse of others. May we be teachable before the Lord, as together we serve the house churches of China.

Part 1

REVISITING THE PAST

DESTINED FOR BITTERNESS

CHAPTER I

I was born into extreme poverty on December 10, 1957, in a southern village of Henan province, China. During that time the government's boasts of agricultural abundance were empty and false. Supposedly, each acre of land could yield many thousands of pounds of harvest, even tens of thousands. There were reports of satellite plantations springing up one after another producing wheat and maize—and even iron and steel! Yet, in reality, the people were constantly hungry, and practically everyone showed symptoms of severe malnourishment. Tens of thousands of people died as a result of this man-made disaster.

In the village where I lived, even all the tree bark had been consumed. According to my mother, there was one instance when she asked someone to buy a few pounds of tree bark so that she could make soup and help us stay alive. Unfortunately, our family got food poisoning, and could not stop vomiting. Mother wept through the night, believing that she would surely die.

"What will happen to this poor child I leave behind?" she thought to herself. My father and paternal grandparents had already died and she was my only caregiver. The next day, however, she amazingly recovered. I remember none of these details, but I do remember that I was not able to walk at three to four years of age due to extreme hunger. Desperate for anything to eat, we scrounged for even the unthinkable. Unforgettable was the taste of wild goose's excrement, a culinary experience that remains vivid to this day.

Almost all my peers died of hunger, and the people in my village said I was like a cat with nine lives since I continued to survive. In our family, mother and I were left to fend for one another, so I had to cling to her all the time. Still, that was an era of the "people's commune," when everyone, regardless of sex or age, worked and food was distributed in proportion to one's labor. Under those dire circumstances, since we needed food to survive, Mother was forced to go out to work. Many times, she would leave the house early in the morning and return only late at night. Locked up in the house all day, I often cried myself to sleep waiting for her at the door. Once I managed to slip through a crack in the wall and I ran everywhere looking for my mother. About two miles out, I accidentally fell into a rice paddy. My uncle from a neighboring village happened to be passing by and saw a little boy sprawled in the field. He automatically rushed over to rescue me, never imagining that it would be his own nephew. From then on, Mother had little choice but to seek remarriage in order to care for me.

The first few years after my mother remarried, relationships within the family were not too bad. With the birth of younger siblings, I gradually became an outsider of sorts because my step-grandfather constantly ill-treated me. I never recall him ever looking at me directly. Each time he saw me, he seemed to be cursing at me. Thus, my juvenile heart developed a sense of hatred and rebelliousness. I hated the heavens. I hated the earth. I hated myself. I hated my family members. And I hated everything around me. My childhood years passed, filled with deep vengefulness.

Not long after I started schooling, the unprecedented Cultural Revolution began in 1966. Communist Party Chairman Mao Zedong launched the ill-conceived, violent revolution in a desperate attempt to wipe out opposition and consolidate political control. During this 10-year period there were massive purges, countless deaths and the devastation of the entire economy. It was a very dark period for the church as Christians were singled out, persecuted severely, wiping out virtually all Bibles and Christian literature in the country and driving the church even further underground There were tremendous family disputes, deep social unrest and even stoppage of classes at school. Every day, we witnessed criticism sessions. I remember seeing a group of people who believed in Jesus being paraded through the streets wearing tall hats with paper labels stuck to their clothes. A huge crowd followed behind cursing and swearing at them. As for me, I too followed, but I did not dare make a sound, because my maternal uncle's family was Christian. Moreover, I had previously learned a few church hymns, so I had a more positive outlook on believers in Jesus. When I was young, my maternal grandmother named me "Victor" because her hope was that I would grow up to be a victorious Christian. Despite having undergone those many years of atheistic, evolutionistic education, my good impression of Christians never faded.

In 1975, toward the end of the Cultural Revolution and my impending graduation from high school, I contracted a debilitating case of rheumatoid arthritis. It caused me great pain and even if there had been adequate treatment available, our family was too poor to afford it. Days seemed like years and each day was filled with tears as I wrestled with thoughts of killing myself. I was utterly devastated and for some reason I deeply hated myself for having been dealt such a bitter fate. I would go for days without saying a word. I was even reluctant to see anyone, even though numerous friends and relatives came to try to comfort me. They advised me to look on the bright side of things, but I choked on their words. I was certain about my destiny and in my heart I felt there was only one solution—death. My days were preoccupied with questions of what method I could use to commit suicide.

As my mother observed this, she suggested, "Why don't you go stay at your uncle's place for a few days? Perhaps you'll feel better after that." I was fully aware of Mother's intentions. She wanted me to visit my uncle so that I would come to believe in Jesus, but I was very resistant. My heart was filled with extreme ideas and I was opposed to anything and everything, so I replied, "I don't wish to go anywhere, neither do I believe in anything. My only belief is that my life has been destined for bitterness." Deep down, I suspected that my family was keeping a close watch on their purse strings, wishing instead to numb my mind through faith in Jesus. In reality, Mother was quite helpless, and because of me, she shed many tears. Yet, at that time my disease was beyond the reach of medical science. All I could do was lie in my bed, suffering and waiting for death to overtake me.

In 1978, matters grew worse. It seemed that bad things were coming in pairs. My mother suddenly fell gravely ill and doctors diagnosed her illness as cancer. Our entire family broke down in tears, desperately wondering what we were going to do. We had already spent everything we could possibly scrape together on my medical bills, and I wasn't even sure I wanted to live! Now Mother had a fatal disease. What a double dose of trouble! Again our family was desperate because we knew we could not go on without Mother. Everyone at home busied themselves visiting our relatives, trying to borrow enough money for Mother's medical treatment. In August of 1979 we spent our last cent and still her health went from bad to worse. Eventually, she couldn't even walk or swallow food. All she could do was await death.

"I wish to visit your uncle," Mother told me. "I want to bid my final farewells to my relatives there." She asked if I would accompany her and I agreed, thinking that Mother would die very soon. I knew that I too had no desire to live any longer, so I might as well join her in her goodbyes.

THE JOURNEY FROM DESPONDENCY TO JOY

My stepfather put this pitiful pair of mother and son on a rickshaw and transported us to my uncle's home, where the entire family was mobilized to carry both of us into their house. At the sight of our wretched condition, they broke into tears and set about to persuade us to believe in Jesus without further delay. Even if we were to die, they reasoned, at least our souls would go to heaven. Perhaps God, in His graciousness, might even decide to heal our physical bodies. They promptly delivered a verbal presentation of the message of the Lord's Gospel. When they had finished, Mother agreed to receive Christ, but I was still half in doubt. Still, out of respect and due to the persistence of our relatives, I too knelt alongside Mother and called upon the Lord for mercy and grace. Thanks to our Lord's graciousness, something miraculous happened. Mother's appetite returned and she was able to eat again. At that time, I thought it was just a momentary reaction out of her excitement or a mere psychological phenomenon, so I paid very close attention. The second day passed, and then the third. Mother's appetite, as well as her state of health, gradually improved with each passing day.

Another interesting fact I observed was that ever since setting foot in my uncle's house, Mother had not taken a single dose of her medication. Yet, within a short time she was completely healed. I had witnessed with my own eyes the work of God, so I started asking my relatives questions concerning the Christian faith. They were unable to provide me with answers, which was extremely intellectually disturbing to me. For instance, I asked them a simple question, "What does hallelujah mean?" One moment they told me, "It means an army sent down from heaven." Then they would change and say, "No, it means to beat up on Satan." They talked about "Jerusalem" but their pronunciation was rather odd (Yelusaleng) and it sounded to me like Yaolousazhong, which means "Shake, leak and sow." So you can see why I was confused. If I asked too many questions, they would accuse me of being proud, while in reality I was hungry and thirsty for the truth. However, I quickly realized that it was unfair to blame them, for none of them had ever seen a physical copy of the Bible, since all Bibles were confiscated and burned during the Cultural Revolution. Even if they had possessed a Bible, it wouldn't have done much good since none of them was literate.

What now? I had clearly witnessed God's power, but it was intellectually difficult for me to accept. Who would be able to answer my questions? I do not remember for sure who it was, but someone told me, "There's a radio station broadcasting out of Hong Kong called the Good Friend Station that tells stories about Jesus." My aunt's house had a radio, so I borrowed it. The radio programs captivated me and at one sitting, I tuned in from 6 o'clock in the evening until much past midnight. For several months in succession, I kept the same routine without pause. I also took careful notes of what I had heard.

From then on, I truly learned that Jesus Christ is the Son of God, humanity's only Savior, who, for the sake of our sin, was crucified on the cross, was resurrected from the dead and then ascended to heaven, thus giving me newness of life. I was so touched that I willingly received Him as my Savior and my life was transformed! Previously, I had lived in great despair, quivering with fear in the shadows of death, but now I had everlasting life. In the past, I had struggled with despondency but now I had a brand-new hope. This face that had been full of tears now became full of laughter, as the joy and peace of Jesus Christ filled my entire being. Whereas a short time earlier I had gone for months without uttering a word, now I was constantly full of thanksgiving, songs and praise. The young man who previously was unwilling to meet anyone now craved for more people to have conversations with, so that he might share with them the benefits of this Good News. My body was no different from before, my health was still bad, but my life had been completely transformed. Each day was spent mesmerized by the wonderful grace of God.

Many of the older Christians in the neighboring villages who had remained true to Christ after the Cultural Revolution rejoiced greatly when they heard about my conversion. They brought their unbelieving sons and daughters to my house, asking me to please explain to them the Gospel message and tell them stories about Jesus. The Holy Spirit worked mightily among us, and believers were daily added by our Lord to His Church.

WEIGHING PRISON FOR A BIBLE

In the summer of 1980, house church meetings in our village were formally established. Initially, our number was under 20 people but by 1982, there were close to 200 attending. After I truly got to know the Lord, He placed the burden of winning souls upon my heart. I was under a lot of pressure, since I had never seen what an evangelist looked like, and there was no complete copy of the Bible for miles around. On top of that, there was a complete lack of reference books. There were so many difficult questions being asked but no one around to answer them. For example: Did man really evolve from apes? If Jesus Christ is truly good news, then why do so many refuse to believe in Him? Why do people say that Christianity is a Western religion? What are the differences between Christianity and other religious faiths? These and numerous other questions had me baffled.

One day I was sitting in the courtyard pondering these issues, wondering how to explain them clearly to others and taking some notes. Suddenly, a 70-year-old lady passed by our house, stepped into our courtyard and asked for a drink. Her words disrupted my stream of thought and when she saw what I was doing, she asked me what I was writing. I replied that it concerned matters of "believing in Jesus."

"Why, I'm a Christian, too!" She introduced herself and told me that she had previously taught at Xian University. She explained that she had remained unmarried out of her devotion to the Lord. I told her, "I have not been a believer for long, so there are many questions bothering me. May I ask you some?" Not only did she answer my questions, she even gave me two booklets, one on "How to Prove God's Existence," and the other on "The Fallacies of Humankind's Evolution from Apes." I joyfully received those booklets, but also told her that I did not have a copy of the Bible.

She said, "I've heard that they can send Bibles in from Hong Kong."

"I've heard about that from the Bible radio, but the authorities consider Gospel radio as the enemy's broadcast. Whoever listens to it is liable for arrest. Can I really obtain a Bible from Hong Kong?"

She encouraged me by saying, "Just give it a try."

I thought to myself "If I have to be imprisoned, then so be it—but I need a Bible." I wrote to the Gospel radio station in Hong Kong and explained to them my deep-felt desire for a Bible. Thanks be to God for answering the prayers of this poor man! A few months later, they actually sent me one and miraculously, I was able to receive it. As I held that copy of the Bible in my hands, tears rolled down my cheeks. It was a dream come true! Finally, I possessed a copy of the Bible. Brothers and sisters in Christ heard about it and traveled from tens of miles around just to behold this sight. We gave thanks together in gratitude to God for meeting the needs of our church.

From then on, we copied every chapter and verse by hand and distributed them to every Christian, exhorting them not only to memorize the Scripture, but also to preach it. The Gospel spread like wildfire throughout the villages and house churches were established everywhere. Revival was upon our churches. It was entirely the working of the Holy Spirit, who authenticated the truth of our preaching with signs and wonders.

In the village where we lived, there were at least four

testimonies of people being raised from the dead along with many other healings. A certain Mrs. Wang was diagnosed with advanced bladder cancer. The hospital refused her treatment and informed her family to come fetch her so that she wouldn't die on her journey home. Her family immediately started preparations for her funeral, but a group of Christians from among us also responded quickly and visited her. We prayed to God on her behalf, asking God to manifest His power and shower His grace upon Mrs. Wang.

While we were praying, many villagers laughed cynically, saying, "If this woman recovers from this illness, our entire village will believe." They had valid reasons for being so skeptical. She had been diagnosed by a top medical doctor from the county hospital who specialized in this type of cancer. However, we ignored their cynicism and told the Lord, "The church needs this elderly lady because she has always demonstrated hospitality to believers. Without her, our church ministry would be crippled." On the third day of our prayer vigil, God answered our prayers and Mrs. Wang fully recovered. "Because of your enemies, our God has ordained praise...from the lips of children and infants...to silence the foe and the avenger." (Psalm 8:2, rearranged).

There was another individual whom I addressed as cousin. He had a severe case of fluid accumulation in his liver. His whole body was seriously swollen, but his family had run out of money for medical treatment. All they could do was await his certain death. Thus, we came and prayed for him. He saw a vision of God saving him, telling him that he would be healed on the second day. Sure enough, he was healed the next day.

Yet another person had cancer. Another had a blood clot in his brain. They, too, were miraculously healed by God. Testimonies like these are too many to number. Under the circumstances, where our village had no pastor or copies of the Bible, God testified for Himself through signs, wonders, and the gifts of the Spirit and the working of His mighty power. True accounts like these can be found in churches all over the country.

THE COUNTER-REVOLUTIONARY ON THE RUN

CHAPTER II

The numerical increase in our church brought about significant social impact. Believing families got along cordially with one another. Faith in Christ resulted in many changes from social ills, such as children who were disobedient to their parents, daughters-in-law who verbally and physically abused their parents-in-law, couples who did not get along, beatings and much more. Moreover, those who believed in Jesus contributed their fair share of agricultural produce to the commune, paid their taxes and helped to support social welfare. In many respects, Christians took the lead in good deeds. At that time, many of the local officials were extremely pleased with the conduct of Christians. On numerous occasions when they could not solve a problem, they would seek the assistance of the Christians.

Unknown to us at the time, things would suddenly take a dramatic shift for the worse. In the spring of 1982, many party officials came to our church and declared our meetings illegal. Those from the religious and security bureaus insisted that we join the Three-Self Patriotic Movement (TSPM). Initially, we were very willing to do so since, essentially, we were already self-governing, self-sustaining and self-propagating. On top of that, we loved our country, so what could be wrong with being part of the TSPM?

We were handed a stack of documents and told to study them carefully. However, the contents shocked us all at first sight. According to the documents, we were mandated to learn and obey the "15 Prohibitions," which were all contrary to the Bible. What now? We put forth some effort in probing the TSPM's background and discovered that they subscribed to a form of "new theology" which paid scant respect to the fundamentals of the Christian faith. I consulted my brothers and sisters in Christ on our appropriate response and they all agreed that we should believe in Jesus, as the Bible says, regardless of what the TSPM taught. We must not cease to meet together and we must continue to rely on our consciences in dealing with both God and man. From that time forward, our meetings were repeatedly disrupted with arrests and interrogations. We had little choice but to adapt and constantly alter our meeting times and locations. Sometimes we would meet in the afternoon, other times at night. Sometimes we would meet in homes, other times we would meet in the wilderness.

On Christmas Day, 1982, more than 300 of us gathered for a meeting. All of a sudden, county and village officials arrived and surrounded our meeting place. A few people were taken away for questioning. Obviously, I was one of their prime targets. Without rhyme or reason, they fired a constant barrage of derogatory words at me for two to three hours. My deep-felt grievances at being wrongfully accused overwhelmed me and I broke into tears that uncontrollably rolled down my cheeks. I prayed, "Oh, Lord! Please behold Your servant's sorry state and silence the arrogant attacks of those who despise You and take Your name in vain!" After I had finished praying, the official who had most vehemently bombarded me with insults suddenly changed his tone: "Only the Lord knows; only the Lord knows." He repeated this about four or five times, and then said nothing else and promptly left the room.

From that time on we were not able to openly meet again. However, our secret meetings multiplied. Brothers and sisters in Christ thirsted and hungered for the Lord's Word more than ever before, and their faith was thereby strengthened. The hope that we all shared also became that much more clear and distinct. I thanked God for His work among His children. Yet, I also knew for sure that we would be facing trials of increasing severity.

In June of 1983, sources from all around indicated that a nationwide series of persecutions was about to begin. We had no choice but to strengthen the believers and prepare ourselves to face the coming trials. All the while, we were praying that the Lord would open a way for us to get through it. I spent those days in itinerant visits throughout the surrounding villages encouraging the hearts of the saints, persuading them to maintain the faith in which they believed, and to prepare to enter the kingdom of God by means of suffering.

On July 5, 1983, I completed my planned itinerary and stayed with a family that loved the Lord. They were always willing to serve and receive visitors. The entire family told me that since my circumstances had changed so drastically, I could stay with them for the long term. They also had made alternate plans and places to hide me so that I could continue to secretly comfort brothers and sisters in Christ to help them be steadfast in persecution. This was a plausible plan, I thought, for I had already weighed the options. I could not return home, because if the security bureau were to dispatch officials there, my step-grandfather would surely hand me over to them. Further, established church groups beyond my area of ministry did not even know who I was. Under such dangerous circumstances, who would be willing to receive me into their homes since they had never met me? It appeared that staying with this family was my only viable option, and so that is what I did.

Right after I made that decision, I started feeling faint and I vomited repeatedly. Fear overcame me, and for the next two days, I was unable to eat anything. I thought I was about to die, or possibly that God wanted to hand me over to the authorities. I told the members of my host family, "Send me away! Perhaps my time has come." When they saw how seriously ill I was, they broke into tears and reluctantly placed me on a rickshaw and took me home. Upon reaching home and lying down in bed, the symptoms of my illness disappeared. My appetite returned and my spirit was back to its former self. I was truly startled, but I still could not figure out why God was dealing with me in this manner. I said to myself, "All right, all I can do is submit to God and His will." Suddenly, Brother Shen Yiping came running to my house and told me, "Security bureau personnel are on their way to get you. Quick! Get up and run!" I told him, "I have nowhere else to go. Maybe God wants me to fall into their hands." I then told him about my recent experiences. He replied, "God's thoughts are higher than our thoughts, so whenever there are obstacles in one place, we will move to another." Brother Yiping wanted me to act immediately and despite my protests, he dragged me out of the house. We went westward and came to the home of a brother where we safely remained for a while but a heavy burden continued to bear down on my heart.

It was only later that I realized the truth. July 9, 1983, was the date set for a large-scale, nationwide operation to arrest house church leaders. On that day, tens of thousands of believers were taken from churches all over the country. As an evangelist from a non-TSPM house church, a warrant of arrest had obviously been issued to get me. During the afternoon of July 9, security bureau officials came to my home, scrutinizing every scrap of paper and then searched thoroughly for miles around. My entire family was interrogated. My step-grandfather, who was never in favor of my believing in Jesus, had little hesitation in revealing all the possible addresses he knew of where I could be hiding. Based on those leads, all the addresses were searched and eventually they came to the host family in whose house I had fallen sick. All the members of that family, from young to old, were called out and questioned. Their house was turned upside down for evidence of my whereabouts. The family members answered the officials truthfully. "He became seriously ill, so we sent him back home." This brought the officials back to my home for another round of interrogation but all my step-grandfather knew was that I had returned home looking desperately sick. He was clueless to whatever happened to me after. I thank God for rescuing me in a way I could never have predicted.

The officials put up posters in various villages and major intersections seeking my arrest. They described me as a counter-revolutionary cloaked in religious garments. They even declared that I was a core member of Witness Lee's Shouters sect. How did they ever come up with that association? I had no idea who Witness Lee was, since I neither had any contact with people outside my sphere of ministry, nor had I read his books or heard his sermons. All I knew was that we were to believe in Jesus, love God, love people, preach the Gospel and perform good deeds. Now I had been branded as a counter-revolutionary. The county in which I was hiding came under investigation, so the church brothers arranged for me to be sent to another county at night. There, I stayed with a distant cousin for three days, but when they heard from other sources about my situation, they were afraid to keep me with them any longer, so I had to leave their house.

PERSECUTION LEADS TO A LAND OF ABUNDANCE

Where could I go now? Who would even dare to receive me? At my wits' end, I reluctantly arrived at my maternal uncle's home. He was hardly pleased to see me since I had intruded upon their privacy unannounced but I had little room to maneuver around the niceties of Chinese courtesy. On account of our family relations, they housed me, but in a building no bigger than about 75 square feet. There, I was "imprisoned" for 29 days. In the summer's heat, I ate, slept and discharged my bowels within the small confines of that room. Besides sleeping, I had little else to do but pray. I was not allowed to meet anyone, but the brothers and sisters in the church had no idea where I was, anyway. The first 20-plus days passed with much peace in my heart, but the final few days were filled with deep-felt turmoil. I thought to myself, "I am an evangelist yet I cannot preach the Gospel. I cannot even read the Bible and no one can receive me into their homes." So I prayed earnestly to God, "I do not wish to wait here for another day. If I have to be a beggar while evangelizing, then so be it. Otherwise, let me go to prison right now, lest I waste my life in this miserable place."

God heard my prayer and answered it two days later. Two teenage sisters in Christ managed to locate my hiding place, which totally shocked me. When I asked them how they found me, they said God had told them to come fetch me. I inquired further, "Where are we going, then?" They replied, "Don't ask too many questions. Just submit."

I was too stunned to inquire any further as the sisters made me lie down on a rickshaw cart and then covered me with a blanket. Not knowing east from west or north from south, I was taken on a three-hour journey before arriving at a place I had never been to before. There, I was warmly received by a family who housed me in one of their rooms with a young little sister. This household of ten were all Christian believers, with the exception of the father.

"Will this work?" I asked. They answered, "No problem. Just entrust all things to the Lord." Yet, I felt uncomfortable because people in our region were especially conservative and would never allow a male to frivolously enter a female's room. How could I explain myself if the father of the house were to find out that I was staying in his young daughter's room? All I could do was to pray to the Lord for deliverance.

On the third day, something amazing happened. Brother Shen Yiping, who had been separated from me for well over a month, discovered my whereabouts, and even found the exact room in which I was staying. I asked him, "How did you possibly find out where I am?" He said, "The Lord led me." I inquired further, "Have you previously been to this village?" He replied, "No. Never."

Brother Yiping went on to recount that since being forced to scatter on July 9, he had run to warn Brother Zhang and Uncle Feng to quickly flee from the authorities. Uncle Feng had previously been sentenced to five years' imprisonment in 1975 because of his Christian faith. True enough, the security bureau officials promptly came to their homes. Together, they all fled to the region of Mount Tongbo. Along the way, they met Brother He, who was much more familiar with Christian contacts in the mountainous areas. Thus, they traveled together to many places and met with numerous members of Christ's body who had likewise been persecuted and forced to flee. They learned about my predicament and agreed to meet with me. Once arrangements had been made, Brother Yiping set off in search of me. When he got to my uncle's house, he learned that two girls had taken me away without telling him where they were taking me. There was not much he could do except pray earnestly for the Lord's leading so that he could find me. He prayed unceasingly and depended on the Holy Spirit for guidance. Without asking a single person for directions, Brother Yiping was led of the Lord and found his way to my precise location. We could not stop praising God with hearts full of thanksgiving for the grace He had shown us.

When nightfall came, we bade farewell to this wonderful family. This was the beginning of an itinerant evangelistic ministry outside the confines of our village. Initially, when we were forced out of our hometown, we could not comprehend why God had allowed this to happen. In the church we were in, the brothers and sisters loved one another in the Lord, and our ministry was only just establishing structure. With the onset of persecution, we lost all that. This frustrated us so much that we even began to complain to God, questioning His arrangements.

One day, while spending time with the Lord, I came across a scripture in Acts.

> *On that day a great persecution broke out against the church at Jerusalem, and all except the apostles were scattered throughout Judea and Samaria.*
> ***Acts 8:1***

The Spirit illumined me as I suddenly realized the relevance of this verse to our situation. Weren't we previously just like the Christians in Jerusalem? It seemed that their hearts were narrow, as they cared only for the establishment of their local ministries to the neglect of Gospel needs beyond their boundaries. They seemed to have scant regard for the Great Commission. Through suffering and persecution, God disrupted the serenity of their comfort zone, much like a mother eagle would disturb her young eaglets from the nest so that they will flex their wings and learn to fly. I confessed before the Lord, "Oh, God, may You forgive me for my folly. Your intention was to test and train us, in the process placing the burden of a broader ministry vision upon our hearts. Despite having undergone a baptism of fire, You have led us into this wonderful land of abundance."

CHURCH GROWTH, CHINESE STYLE–TWENTY BELIEVERS TO 30,000 IN TWO YEARS

At the end of the Cultural Revolution, there remained a group of older Christians around 70 years of age. Most of them did not know the Bible very well, but all of them had great hearts for the Lord. They kept their daily prayer vigils and lived pious lives. We visited some of these older believers and explained to them the biblical message of salvation through Jesus Christ. Through them, we had opportunities to evangelize their grandchildren and other relatives, as well. Those who were exceptionally eager to learn underwent more intensive training. We unloaded the little biblical truths that we knew on them, and encouraged them to take up responsibility for the church and the Gospel mandate. God's Spirit worked mightily in our midst. From relative to relative and friend to friend, our Gospel ministry continued to grow and expand. Many who were sick received healing. Criminals repented. Families with disputes started living in harmony. Those who were disappointed with life and living in despondency found their burdens lifted from their hearts because of salvation through Jesus Christ. Hearts were comforted and satisfied. Wherever our church's brothers and sisters went, God's Word spread like wildfire.

I remember a certain village in Wangji, where I had Bible study with the villagers for 19 consecutive nights. The number of attendees gradually increased until eventually, the house was filled both inside and out. They busily took notes on their little booklets. It was then the autumn harvest season, the busiest time of the agricultural calendar. Despite their many responsibilities and tight schedules, the fervent hearts within these tired bodies would not allow them to rest in their homes. A certain Sister Bi shared with me that she hardly slept a wink for those 19 nights. Each night, as the meetings ended around 1 or 2 o'clock in the morning, she would return home to slice sweet potatoes and feed the cows. Before daybreak, she had to be in the fields for harvesting. Still, she happily told me, "God's grace is truly amazing. As your days are, so will your strength be. He is indeed our ever present help."

Since the brothers and sisters had a strong desire for the truth, we kept increasing the number of meetings. God raised up for us many families who were willing to receive and host itinerant preachers out of service to our Lord. This flexibility of meeting in different homes brought us much-needed convenience. Hence, we called them "home meetings."

At the end of 1984, we had established more than 200 host families. Due to a lack of pastoral personnel, we had an immense workload. During that time, circumstances were somewhat better than before, so we busily conducted meeting after meeting, nonstop. When evening came, the believers from the villages would swarm toward the designated meeting point, before they even had time to have dinner. Each meeting saw attendances in the hundreds. This was also when many God-loving parents dedicated their children to the Lord. After receiving training, these people became part of the evangelistic teams. The fire of evangelistic fervor swept across many of the surrounding cities and towns.

Then some of our members began to evangelize in the provinces of Hubei and Anhui. We were also invited to Xinyang. An elderly lady called Old Aunt He had visited our hometown and when she realized that we were preaching about Jesus Christ, her heart was exceedingly moved. She told us that before 1949, she had believed in Jesus through the ministry of foreign missionaries. Not long thereafter, those missionaries were forced to leave Chinese soil and she had not seen a preacher preach since. All she could do was keep her faith to herself. However, in the past two years, many people had come knocking on her door wanting to believe in Jesus. Some brought the sick and demon-possessed and even animals, asking for her prayer on their behalf. Through her prayers, healings occurred. Yet, she had hardly any Bible knowledge, and was not able to bring anyone to Christ, so she invited us to go help her. We all said, "This is the Macedonian call!"

That is how we decided to do evangelism in Xinyang with Old Aunt He. Upon arriving there, we gathered to her house all those who had already had a foretaste of God's grace, and told them, "We believe in God, the Maker of heaven and earth. He loves us, and sent His son Jesus Christ to this world to save sinners. Through the many miracles and wonders He has performed among you, Jesus has evidenced that He is the Son of God that we may believe in Him and receive life in His name." We meticulously explained to them the Gospel message, and exhorted them to share it with those around them. The Holy Spirit was at work in their midst, and the church there was quickly established. Old Aunt He had the spiritual gift of healing and casting out demons, so we ministered alongside her throughout the region of Xinyang.

People residing in the mountainous areas were very fond of visitors. Whenever we went to their homes, they would gladly receive us. One day, a certain brother and I arrived at one such home. The head of this household warmly received us and once he realized the purpose of our visit, he invited his neighbors. Upon hearing the gospel message, about 20 of them expressed their desire to accept Jesus as their personal Savior. Immediately, they knelt down in prayer and just like that, a meeting place was established. Next, we followed them to their relatives' homes. In this manner, the Gospel was spread throughout that area and within two years, more than 30,000 people trusted in Jesus. As a consequence, our names were blacklisted by the security bureau.

Our next stop was in Queshan County in the region of Zhumadian, where we preached in a few villages to the west of that city. God was our co-worker. He performed miracles through us as we bore witness to His word. As we gathered, the parents of Brother Zhang's 23-year-old nephew brought their son to the meeting. The accumulation of fluids in his liver was so bad that he could not even button up his father's pants that he was wearing. They had returned from the hospital in utter despondency. Since there seemed to be no other way for their son to get well, they decided to bring him to our meeting. After our second day of meetings, this young man's health was completely restored. People had come from all around for our meeting and after hearing us preach the Gospel of Jesus Christ, they brought this piece of good news home with them.

After more than a month, we returned to visit the places where we had previously evangelized. The brothers and sisters in one area wanted to take us to the eastern side of the city for ministry.

"Who first preached the gospel here?" we asked.

They answered, "You did."

"No, you must be mistaken," I said. "This is my first visit to this area."

They replied, "We are certainly not mistaken. Remember the last time you came? Was there not a Brother Liu with a tape recorder? He lives here, and he brought back tape recordings of your messages and played them in these villages. Thus, many people have come to faith in Jesus. In just over one month, 25 churches have been established here."

Upon hearing that, I was deeply moved, and I told them, "It wasn't me. It was God. Behold! How earnest God is for the welfare of His people!"

May God have mercy on us! May He remember our needs! It is true,

> *The harvest is plentiful but the workers are few.*
> ***Matthew 9:37***

On this road of ministry that we travel, there are times of rejoicing and celebration, but there are also times of suffering and tears. I remember when I first left home, my mother cut my hair very short, so that in case I was arrested, it would be more difficult for the officials to grab hold of my hair and throw me to the ground. Due to my disabilities, she knew that it would be difficult for me to get up by myself if I fell down. Thus, for the first ten years of my ministry, I kept my hair length as short as possible.

We brothers often reminded one another, "As evangelists, we must always be ready to go to jail." Prior to every meeting, we would carefully hide our books. We would loosen the buttons on our collars in the event we were caught so that if they grabbed our shirts, it would be harder for them to choke us. The lyrics to one of our favorite songs went, "During apostolic times when the blood of martyrs flowed like rivers, death was not chief among their concerns. Tens of thousands have made sacrifices for the sake of the Gospel. I too am willing to lay down everything and be a martyr for the Lord."

Our most common sermon topics were "Self-denial, Suffering, Carrying Your Cross, and Evangelizing." We understood that to follow Jesus was to enter into a way of suffering. Without a heart totally dedicated to the Lord, it is very difficult for one to persevere till the end. When I first left home, I was very innocent at heart. I made a resolution before God that for three years I would not step back into my own house. Even secular achievements require tremendous resolution and determination, much less the Lord's ministry. How can a person on whom God has shown grace not be willing to pay the price for the Lord's sake?

Before 1990, standards of living in the villages were especially low. There were very few times when we got to eat three meals a day. Often, we would go many days without a shower. The clothes we wore during the day became our blankets during the night. Sometimes we would sleep in the open fields, and other times we would rest in cowsheds. We met people who lovingly received us into their homes, but we also faced cruel rejection. Such a lifestyle caused many of us itinerant evangelists to have lice on our bodies. Once when we co-workers gathered together, out of boredom, we started to pick lice off of each other. Some had a few hundred, but the least among us had a few dozen. One brother noticed that the lice on our bodies were huge and fat, so he jokingly said, "Let me bring brushes and knives to help you." Everyone thought that was hilarious and we laughed uproariously. Even in hardship, we knew great joy.

Although life was somewhat difficult, Jesus Christ was the greatest source of joy and satisfaction in our hearts. We constantly reminded one another of our status as God's servants. It was our objective as much as possible to minimize the burdens we placed on the brothers and sisters, lest our Lord's name be disgraced as a result. The last thing we wanted was to allow those opposed to God a license to indict us, and instead, that at the day of reckoning, glory be given unto God.

The political climate in China is unpredictable. One day it may be sunny and pleasant, but the next day may bring a thunderstorm. Whatever the case may be, we need only to maintain a heart purely devoted to loving our Lord that we may overcome—be it in times of wealth or poverty, whether well fed or hungry, in need or in plenty, in life or in death. Despite the ever-changing circumstances around us, God protected us time and time again.

One time we came to the home of a Brother Li. About 70 to 80 brothers and sisters came from afar to see me, and we had a wonderful time of fellowship in God's Word. As we were preparing for lunch, I suddenly had this strange inclination and murmured, "Let's have lunch in the inner room." The host family was perplexed by my unusual request because the inner room was too small to house that many people. It was barely 10′ x 12′ and half the space was already taken up by wheat stacks. Moreover, there was a bed in the room, which belonged to the daughter of the house. The family members said nothing, but their facial expressions revealed their displeasure. They sat down to eat in the dining room, while we guests squeezed ourselves into that tiny room, with many of us sitting in awkward positions. When we were ready to eat, a squad of officials suddenly stormed the house after having been tipped off by a local. Upon entering the house, all they saw was the family having lunch in their dining hall. Nothing appeared to be amiss, so after sitting down for a while, they left.

On another occasion, Brother Shen Yiping and I went together to a mountainous area for itinerant evangelism. Because we had several meetings to attend on Sunday, we decided to split up. At daybreak, we came to a particular place, and the brothers and sisters were also gradually arriving for the meeting. Within minutes, the wind started gusting, dark clouds filled the sky, and it began to rain heavily. I was about to commence preaching, when the two top-level village officials arrived and parked themselves at the door. They began reading aloud the Xinyang regional documents, and later the county committee's documents. I sensed that they were after me, for the contents of these documents matched my previous charges, "leader of the sect, here to mesmerize and mislead the people, with intentions of instigating counter-revolutionary activities." They advised the people present not to be deceived by my lies. Should they find out the whereabouts of this person, they said, they would immediately report him to the security bureau. I thought to myself, "I am standing right before your eyes, but your charges are absolutely false. No matter what you say, these brothers and sisters know what I believe in and what I preach."

When they had finished reading their documents, the officials started recording the names of all the attendees. A group of brothers signaled for me to lie down on the bed. When it came my turn, the brothers told them, "He is not feeling well. He needs rest." The officials did not inquire further. They led a few co-workers away and promptly left. After that, I got up, encouraged and strengthened the believers, and then quickly ended the meeting for that day. I had just sat myself down in the kitchen when those officials came back again, wanting to find out the identity of that man who was lying on the bed a while ago. Someone told them, "Well, as you can see, he isn't there anymore." They searched all over the house, but somehow God did not allow them to step into the kitchen. Once the officials left, we too decided to leave. About ten minutes after we left, the officials returned to the house, this time searching the kitchen as well. Hallelujah! God is aware of our weaknesses and He takes us under the shadow of His protecting wings, that we may elude the nets of poachers.

THE SPIRIT'S FIRE IGNITES THE CHURCH

As of 1988, churches were consistently established through active propagation of the Gospel in various regions, and hunger for truth gradually increased. Around 1989, foreign teachers came to China proclaiming messages concerning the "filling of the Holy Spirit." Among us, approximately one third accepted the teaching, another third objected, while the remainder maintained an attitude of caution. I knew that being filled by the Spirit is a scriptural truth and also something the church needs. Personally, I yearned to be filled by the Spirit, but I was ignorant of what true Spirit-filling entailed, so I accepted this teaching with fear and trembling. Certain teachers from abroad came and laid their hands on me, but there was no response on my part. All I could do was carefully examine Scripture, taking special note of how people experienced Spirit-filling, while consulting related books and perusing the annals of church history. I pled with the Lord not to leave me out of the floods of His Spirit's filling. Simultaneously, I tried to be as careful and discerning as I could, so that I would not be deceived by others. I persistently prayed before God concerning this important matter. A year later, I was praying in a ravine when I was filled with the Spirit. My heart was flooded with peace and joy. After that experience, added strength was given me to serve the Lord. My vision for ministry was renewed, and I began to understand many more truths that were previously alien to me.

Through this lighting of the Spirit's fire of revival, church ministries also rapidly expanded. The Spirit stirred everyone's heart to love the Lord. The atmosphere in the church was no longer dull. Those who had no desire to pray now prayed through the night in tears. Attendance rose at our meetings. Moreover, even when meetings had officially ended, the brothers and sisters were reluctant to leave for home. Everyone endeavored to exercise their spiritual gifts, be it evangelism, healing, exorcism, preaching or praise and worship. Members were striving for positions of ministry, and the church was filled with a harmonious spirit of love, joy and peace. We not only studied the Bible constantly, but also reminded everyone to maintain a balance between reason and experience, spiritual life and spiritual gifts, knowledge and spiritual empowerment, rationality and spirituality, substance and numbers. We strove to follow our Lord, turning neither to the left nor to the right.

I observed that many local churches went to dangerous extremes in their practices. Some furiously opposed Spirit-filling and especially placed emphasis on theological training. Others exalted Spirit-filling while neglecting thorough equipping in biblical truth. Extremists in both camps clashed, even to the extent of attacking and charging one another of heresy. This often resulted in church splits and enmity among brother sand sisters, all in the name of earnestly contending for and defending the truth. Unknowingly, they had fallen into Satan's snares. Churches ought to foster mutual respect and learn from one another. My vision, mission and ministry direction is to focus on our common goal for evangelistic ministry.

FIRST IMPRISONMENT – "YOU WILL DIE IN PRISON"

The summer of 1992 was extremely warm. River flows were disrupted, the ground cracked due to dryness, and agriculture withered. Farming communities, which depended on heaven's blessings of suitable weather, had their hearts burdened with worry as they considered the state of their fields and the bleak outlook for that year's harvest. Our meetings continued unabated, although we were especially cautious, since our brothers and sisters were consistently being arrested. Hence, instead of holding large gatherings, we opted for small group meetings. Some members warned me to be careful, but I joked with them, "May the Lord have mercy on me, and keep me from going to prison this time of the year. The weather is simply too warm. I don't think I can take it." A few days later, while meeting at Brother Yin's place, Public Security Bureau officials came and sealed off all exits to the house. More than 90 members and I were promptly taken away to the local police station. I was locked up for the night in a tiny cell with a floor area of 12 square feet. The next day, they interrogated me under torture, and were ready to transfer another brother and me to the county prison. The rest of our members were fined and then released.

When the Chief Cui of the county's Public Security Bureau learned of my arrest, he could not control his elation and personally drove me to prison, with sirens blaring. On the way, he told me with delight, "It took me so many years to find you. This time, there will be no turning back. You will surely die in Xidagang (the detention prison)." I silently prayed to the Lord for His guidance. As I entered the prison, I saw a large group of jaundiced and scrawny-looking prisoners, each with bare bodies and wearing only a pair of shorts. Even their shorts were often worn through and their bottoms showed through the holes. It was all a scary sight. As I stood among them, they repeatedly "interrogated me." Finally, they concluded, "Believers in Jesus are good people." I was allowed to sit in a designated space along the row of wooden beds. This was where I would eat, drink, sit and sleep. About three feet away from me were two urinal containers. Since our daily diet consisted mainly of congee (rice broth), each person would urinate many times a night. Before daybreak, the urinals would overflow, covering the floor area in and around my designated spot. It was just about unbearable.

Due to the extreme heat and scarcity of rainfall, the water we consumed was fetched from the river. Each bowl of rice contained numerous insects and worms. Hygiene was an entirely alien concept for us. After each meal, we would all sit neatly in rows. If the guards saw anything disorderly through the gaps in the walls, violators would be beaten almost to death.

Under those circumstances, I had no physical copy of the Bible. All I could do was meditate on the verses I had memorized and silently pray to God for strength to overcome the suffering. God granted me a pure heart, so that I never desired an early release from prison. If such thoughts surfaced, I immediately prayed for God to strengthen and preserve my resolve, so that I would not seek an easy way out. I kept very quiet. One day, a prison mate with some level of education approached me and commented, "I have been observing you these past few days. I can tell that you are different from others. Most people will either weep or make a fuss, but you are so quiet. It seems to me that your heart manages to seek refuge beneath the shade of trees from the intense heat of summer. What is your secret?" I showed him my piece of broken hand fan, on which I had written, "Peace of heart makes even a hut steady. Resolution of emotions makes even vegetable roots savory. In all things, turn your eyes upon the Lord. At all times, trust in God." Through this short poem, I shared God's Word with him. He was very moved, and began to understand many truths.

For half a month in prison, the Public Security officials never interrogated me. A day past half a month, they questioned me for only 30 minutes. Only later did I realize that Chief Cui, the man who had personally driven me to prison, was fired from his position on the third day after I entered prison because he had committed some grave error on the job. Truly the Lord protected me! Thanks be to God, Chief Cui's prediction that I would "not return and surely die in Xidagang" went unfulfilled. After more than three months of imprisonment, I was released.

During those three-plus months, I gained a deeper appreciation for the futility of legislation and the utter depravity of sinful humanity. Evildoers shamelessly passed down their "techniques" of sinful behavior. The detention prison was basically a tank of pollution where those without sin became sinners, and minor offenses were magnified. The government is ignorant that Christians are their true comrades and friends in maintaining public order and combating evil. Yet, how will they ever understand Christians?

EMISSARIES SENT THROUGHOUT CHINA

CHAPTER III

As church ministry expanded, house meetings developed into local churches. Brothers and sisters who were forced to leave their homes repeatedly formed alliances with one another. In this manner, a form of team ministry gradually took shape that we called "united missions." I remember a certain brother saying, "All of us walk this same path because of our faith in Jesus and our desire to preach the Gospel. We are a gospel fellowship." Thus, the label "Gospel Fellowship" became widely used although a gospel fellowship on a smaller scale had already taken shape in 1983 (known outside China as China Gospel Fellowship).

In spring 1994, more than a hundred co-workers gathered at Tanghe to send off a group of young brothers and sisters who had joined our evangelistic ministry. The following phrase in large letters was prominently displayed at the front of our meeting place: "To proudly soar on wings of eagles, and not hide like swallows underneath the eaves." With vibrant singing of hymns, the commissioning ceremony began. "Oh, Lord, may You lead us by the hand through stormy weather. Oh, Lord, may You guide our hearts, that we may fly to the ends of the earth. May these elite troops of Your army go forth from this place, and may the fire of the good news spread through mountain high and valley low, to all four corners of the globe. Some day, China will see true revival!" Subsequently, there was prayer and praise, a commissioning speech, a roll call, exhortation from the leaders, expositional preaching and sharing by a few representatives. The ceremony concluded with words of benediction. Brothers embraced brothers, and sisters embraced sisters, as we reluctantly bade farewell to one another with tears rolling down our cheeks. Seventy "Gospel emissaries" were voluntarily dispatched to more than 20 provinces throughout the country. Their main tasks were:

1. Pioneer gospel preaching
2. Revive dormant churches
3. Unite brother churches
4. Assist small and weak churches
5. Resist errors of heresy
6. Manifest the Lord's mighty love

A year later, the results were fruitful and we better understood the situation in various parts of the country. The Gospel was preached, churches were established, our network was expanded, and we learned so much. Every person's life and ministry witnessed growth. In particular, two young sisters, whose combined age was barely 40 years, went to Inner Mongolia. Moved by the Lord's love, they volunteered themselves with willing hearts and set out, not knowing exactly where they were to go. Even though they had maps, they had to depend completely upon the guidance of the Holy Spirit. Miracles and wonders followed them as they brought the good news to thousands of families. When I visited them later, it was evident that they were drastically different from when they were first dispatched. They had grown in wisdom and stature, and also in favor with both God and people. When they were preparing to return home, the brothers and sisters to whom they had ministered were reluctant for them to leave, and even accompanied them for a few thousand miles on the journey home.

These sisters have an amazing testimony. The people in Inner Mongolia knew only that they were named Xile and Xiaozhe, and they were from Tanghe. Other than that, they knew nothing. The brothers and sisters from Inner Mongolia wanted to find the young women and make contact with them once again. Now Tanghe is the largest county in Henan Province, so how could they ever locate these two sisters?

The brothers and sisters went to the county train station and inquired of a certain lady, "Do you know this girl named Xiaozhe? She believes in Jesus and preached the Gospel to us. We are here to look for her, but are not sure where she lives." The lady understood their question, and replied, "I'm the only Christian in this train station. In fact, I am the only person in this city who knows that Xiaozhe went to Inner Mongolia, because I dispatched her there myself. And I am also the only person who knows where she is right now. She is in a town a few hundred miles from here conducting a meeting. I had originally planned on attending the meeting, but something serious happened at my home, so I couldn't go. I am the only person who knows the answer to your question, but I will tell you." Upon hearing this, the brothers and sisters from Inner Mongolia were filled with thanksgiving to God for His guidance, and happily set off the few hundred miles to meet Xiaozhe.

At a testimonial service in December 1994, brothers and sisters from all over the country gathered for a time of celebration. We shared about how the Lord had guided us, cared for us, protected us, and how we had experienced God and His miraculous ways. Others also shared about how they had been rejected and had to find lodging on the streets. We talked about various ministries, going many days without food, attacks by enemies, and how we had escaped the devil's clutches. The various testimonies brought tears to our eyes. During those three days, we wept, laughed, prayed, praised, had fellowship and listened to God's Word. Everyone was fully blessed by God's grace and we went our way deeply encouraged.

With the expansion of our mission field, our members were given opportunity to exercise their gifts. Gradually, each person's ministerial role became more evident. Each played his or her role in sharing the burden for the larger good. God allowed us to labor together in complementary fashion. In Christ, we were one body and we functioned as one body, complemented one another, were dedicated to one another, and ministered to one another.

NO HOUSE, NO MONEY, SICK AND PERSECUTED— "WILL YOU MARRY ME?"

Since leaving home in 1983 until 1994, I had been away for more than a decade. With the passage of time, brothers and sisters had gradually aged, some even beyond the usual marriageable age. Still, everyone maintained a heart purely devoted to ministry, and found no time to consider such matters. However, we had one major concern: for all of us to remain unmarried would not be biblical, because singleness is a gift from God, and obviously not everyone has been given such a gift. Should this phenomenon continue, we might eventually become suspect in the eyes of our affiliated brethren. This, in turn, would not only hinder the advance of the Gospel, but also create a stumbling block to future generations of "Gospel emissaries." Furthermore, the fact that some brothers and sisters felt tempted in this area made this issue of marriage even more pressing.

Our co-workers conversed with one another to see how each viewed marriage. Some felt that God had given them the gift of singleness, others wanted a few more years of singleness so as to better focus on the Lord's ministry, while still others could not find suitable marriage partners. There were also the crowd followers who would simply do what everybody else did. In the end, we explained to everyone what the Bible had to say with regard to marriage: it is holy, established by God, and important in His eyes. When considering marriage, each of us must be sure that we were following biblical principles as well as the Lord's leading in our lives. Through a process of getting acquainted, knowing one another, covenanting and promise-making, we then would legally enter marital bliss. Once brothers and sisters had a clear understanding of the question on marriage, they prudently sought their life partners. Someone has described love as a brand of fire that may warm your heart or burn your house down. Which is which is hard to tell.

On this matter of marriage, I prayed to God, asking Him to prepare for me according to His will a sister who was in the faith, virtuous, loving, intelligent, wise and considerate, so that she may assist me in better serving the Lord. In the summer of 1994, I got to know my wife at a co-workers' meeting in Xinyang. She was then a lay believer who helped prepare meals for that meeting, but we were merely acquaintances. In the winter of 1995, I was hospitalized in Xinyang when I met her yet again, so we got to know each other a little better. Each time I prayed or meditated, it was clear to me that she was the partner God had prepared for me. God also caused a Bible verse to repeatedly flash before my mind:

> *Houses and wealth are inherited from parents, but a prudent wife is from the Lord.*
>
> ***Proverbs 19:14***

However, I did not verbally discuss this with her, since I realized that it was a serious matter. Moreover, we were socially so conservative that it was difficult for me to articulate my feelings.

On the night before my scheduled departure from the hospital, a brother who was ministering to me suddenly fell ill, which made him fall into a deep sleep. Due to my disabilities, I could not go anywhere if not for the humble service of this sister. This was the final chance God had prepared for us. We exchanged personal views on marriage and I told this sister, "Based on the standards of this world, I have no credentials. I have neither a permanent roof over my head nor land to till. My body is full of infirmities and I have no money. Furthermore, I am constantly being persecuted. I hope you will seriously consider the implications involved."

"I have long thought about these consequences," she replied. She was willing to use her savings in support of my ministry, and even do some business to help meet my needs. It was only later that she revealed to me God's clear guidance in her decision to marry me. A few months earlier, she had attended a meeting I was conducting. When she saw me, God seemed to say to her, "Marry this man." She immediately ran to another room and said: "Oh, Lord! This must be a mistake. This can never be. In every respect I can think of, there is such a huge disparity between us." In the days that followed, each time she opened her lips to pray, she would instinctively ask, "Oh, Lord! Please grant me a willingness to submit and sacrifice." Whenever she felt willing to submit, a spirit of joy would fill her. Whenever she was reluctant, inexpressible pain would grip her heart. She realized that she was choosing a difficult path requiring steep demands. After a long time of prayer, and after receiving a few signs of confirmation from the Lord, she willingly submitted because she distinctly knew that it was God's will.

When I disclosed our plans to my co-workers, those who knew her well were very much in approval. Thus, things were finalized. In the springtime of 1996, we were married. On our wedding day, there were neither carriages nor a bridal veil; no firecrackers, no banquet, and no bridal bedroom. Two co-workers from church escorted her to a host family, where church elders conducted a simple wedding ceremony for us. Amidst prayers and blessings, we became man and wife. We had no idea where to spend our wedding night, so a co-worker suggested that the only available option was to use the church. On our first night, we still had two beds complete with blankets. On the second night, because there were guests in town, we were down to one bed with cotton quilts. On the third day, due to ministry needs, we were no longer together. We subsequently rented a room in the village where life was much simpler. I recall that during summertime, if we were to purchase a watermelon, we would eat the flesh within and then cook the skin as a vegetable dish. Over time, due to malnutrition, my wife fell seriously ill and we spent over a hundred dollars on medication, which was an extreme financial hardship for us. Circumstances forced us to return to Xinyang, where she could run a business and ease our financial burdens.

Eventually my wife and I were able to settle down and then bad news came. In August 1996, we were told that one of our meeting points in the city had been raided and all our items confiscated. To make matters worse, Uncle Feng, Brother Xing, Brother Zhang and Sister Luo had been arrested and imprisoned. Since I had just started a family, I was not with them, and so I escaped this ordeal.

Early in the spring of 1997, my wife became pregnant. Ministry-wise, we were exceptionally busy because many of our church members had been imprisoned and we had to make up for the work they would normally do. This meant I had to go on itinerant visits to various churches, which required that I be away from home for tens of days at a time. My wife's body did not react very well to her pregnancy, so by the time I got home from my first trip, she could hardly move and was essentially reduced to skin and bones. How rash of me not to have been more sensitive in caring for her needs! I still feel guilty whenever I think about it.

Due to changes and increased pressure, we received more

and more reports of brothers and sisters being arrested. My wife had to confine herself to a little house, lest she give away our location. Still, her whereabouts eventually became known and she had to flee to another home. When I came home from a trip and reached the house where I thought she would be, she was nowhere to be found. Although I knew she was somewhere in Xinyang, I couldn't locate her. All I could do was stay with a host family and await news on her whereabouts. However, she learned where I was and once it was dark, she left her hiding place in the forest and ran to the same host family where I was. We did not know where else we could go. Just then, we received a letter asking us to promptly return home for the government's routine planned pregnancy inspection. By dawn, we had rented a car and left Xinyang.

EASTERN LIGHTNING CULT MUTILATES BELIEVERS

After we reached Tanghe, we heard that the Eastern Lightning cult had become widespread, persistently pestering the various churches with their false teachings. I left my wife at a sister's house, and rushed to visit the churches affected in a bid to salvage believers who had been misled. After a few days of teaching them the truth and exhorting them with God's love, I managed to win back some believers. Within a few days, however, the Eastern Lightning counterattacked. They fractured the lower limbs of four Christians who opposed their "female Christ" and horrendously mutilated them by cutting off their ears and slitting their mouths. A few other brothers and sisters and I were included on their blacklist for a planned backlash. I could not believe my eyes when I visited those Christians at the hospital and I advised them to report this atrocity to the Public Security Bureau. Apart from utilizing legal means, it would be almost impossible for us to combat such cultic behavior. The Eastern Lightning had a dictum: "With persistence, even dripping water can penetrate a rock, and ants can crumble bones. If need be, we shall be shameless and ruthless." Unless we reported them to the authorities, they may enter our homes and simply refuse to leave. We would then have little choice but to feed and house them, hence condoning and encouraging their wicked ways.

However, we had a serious dilemma. Would the Public Security Bureau understand our predicament? We were already their targets as well. And further, even if the officials wanted to arrest the Eastern Lightning, it would be difficult because their meetings were usually clandestine and well planned. Moreover, the Public Security Bureau did not know the difference between truth and heresy. The true church would not resort to violence when opposing heretics, so we decided to continue to pray, preach and try to prevent.

After a period of struggle, we arranged for a three-day meeting in the western part of Henan province, discussing some of the strategies of the Eastern Lightning. On the second day, I told the co-workers that I had to leave because my wife was due for delivery, but they could not bear to let me go. I had to secretly creep away and I arrived home when it was already dark. My wife was writhing in bed from labor pains, so I immediately rushed her to the hospital. Just past 7:00 am on November 1, 1997, I became father to a daughter. I was delighted! We recalled memories of how God's love had enveloped us, and how wave upon wave of His divine grace had blessed our lives. In commemoration of God's love and grace, we named our baby daughter Enbo, meaning "waves of grace."

TORTURE AND FORCED LABOR – A NORMAL LIFE

CHAPTER IV

On November 6, 1997, five days after my daughter was born, I was invited to Xinyang in Henan province to lecture on the evils of the Eastern Lightning. I arrived at the house that I had previously rented, for a change of clothes. As I left the house, I noticed a vehicle labeled "News Reporter" blocking the roadway. Later, I found out that it was a Public Security vehicle that had been monitoring me from across the street. Brother He from Xinyang and I were taken away to the regional police headquarters where we underwent beatings and harsh interrogations throughout the night. On the second day, we were transported to the detention prison.

The authorities located the phone number of a believing family and told them that Brother He and I were involved in a car accident and were now at the Intensive Care Unit of Hospital 154. They told them to come pay for the medical treatment we critically needed. With hearts so pure and innocent, these brethren never suspected anything amiss, and immediately rushed to the hospital with their cash. They were promptly searched, beaten, verbally harassed and arrested. The authorities took all the money from the more than ten people who came, including earrings belonging to Brother He's daughter. Worse still, they found information concerning our meeting point with one of the brothers.

After several months, we realized that terrible tribulation was about to descend upon the churches of Xinyang. On July 7, the Public Security Bureau mobilized their attack squad and surrounded the meeting place. More than one hundred of our co-workers were arrested and imprisoned in different locations. They were individually interrogated and then sentenced according to the "severity of the crimes."

At this time, some peculiar happenings occurred. The Public Security official from Nanwan village of Xinyang county in charge of confiscating items from house churches had taken a full truckload of belongings from the Christians on the night of July 7. This usually responsible official was planning for more confiscations the next morning, July 8, but he felt too tired to do more.

In the village of Paifang, some miles from Xinyang county, something strange also happened on an isolated mountain ridge where a family of four resided. The head of the household, surnamed Hu, was a new believer in Christ. He was a retired professional soldier, paralyzed from the waist down. Many of his comrades at war now held positions in the Public Security Bureau and he watched them attaining prestige and wealth. He had to watch his wife and children working in the fields and he bemoaned the fact that he was a burden to his family. The more he thought about it, the worse he felt. One day when no one else was around, he was overcome by his weaknesses and cut his wrists to end his life. Upon discovering her husband, his wife wept uncontrollably over his sudden death.

At night, about 20 of Brother Hu's former comrades-at-war (now mostly Public Security officials) arrived in five small-sized vehicles for the funeral wake. These men had previously pledged to one another that should any of them ever end up in crisis or need, the others must share the burden with financial contributions. The amazing thing was no one had dispatched any news to them. Mysteriously, they had received the same news on their pagers or cell phones, so they all went to Brother Hu's residence. After donating some money and offering a few words of comfort, they left.

No one was prepared for what happened next. After everyone had left his house, Brother Hu miraculously sat up on his bed. He was apparently healthy and in very good spirits.

"I have seen the Lord Jesus!" he exclaimed. "He told me that some of our brothers and sisters in the house churches have been arrested. They are currently being held at the town of Pingqiao and He wants me to get help and rescue them."

His family members, although joyous that he was alive, were unaware of what had already happened at the church, so they were suspicious of Brother Hu's proclamation. They inquired of the county church and also shared about their recent experiences. The brothers and sisters there were also in doubt, so they conveyed the information on to Brother Shen Yiping at Tanghe.

On the seventh day after Brother Hu was revived from the dead, Brother Shen came from hundreds of miles away to visit the Hu family. Once Brother Shen had verified the truth of the miracle, he told Brother Hu, "Since the Lord Jesus has raised you from the dead, whatever He has commanded you to do, you better do it." So Brother Hu sought out his Public Security friends and testified concerning his resurrection from death and what the Lord Jesus has said to him. Everyone was amazed, and everyone they asked for help agreed to assist. Subsequently, brothers and sisters were successively released, leaving only about ten people who were later sent to the Corrective Labor Facility.

BEATINGS AND STARVATION FAIL TO FORCE US TO FORSAKE CHRIST

Personally, I was held at the detention prison for a total of forty days. When I first entered that place, the atmosphere was extremely tense and they guarded me with special vigilance. I was locked up with about ten other prisoners. The Public Security officials took away whatever money I had and there was not even a scrap of paper in my possession. This resulted in the demeaning necessity of my having to use my hands to clean myself after emptying my bowels. For the first half a month or so, no one was able to send me any clothes or blankets. It was already November and the room was chilled and more humid than usual. At night, lying on the hard wooden planks, I was extremely cold and very miserable.

On the second day of my imprisonment, we could see through the gaps of our jail cell and watched many brothers and sisters escorted in and distributed to various cells. As the days passed, I would hear the guards calling out names of

Christians for interrogation. I had no idea how each person was doing, nor did I know what kind of situation the church was in at that time. Honestly speaking, I had no peace in my heart, and it felt terrible.

A few days after I was imprisoned, Brother Wang was transferred into my cell. From him, I learned about how certain brothers and sisters had been arrested. He told me that he had been interrogated twice. After they forced him to remove all his clothes, they turned the ceiling fan on to full speed. The rush of cold air penetrated to his bones, causing unbearable pain—but it left no bodily scars.

"Why are they so brutal toward believers in Jesus?" I asked.

He answered with a question for me. "Every person has been questioned at least a couple of times. Why haven't you been questioned?"

I replied, "The logic is quite simple. In order to fell a tree, you need to dig and remove the soil from all around the tree. Once you're done with the digging, the tree will naturally fall by itself. They are probably saving me for last. Through the testimonials that they will try to forcibly obtain from interrogating the others, they hope to convict me with a death sentence." Yet, I myself knew that apart from believing in Jesus and evangelizing, I had not done anything illegal. They were just trying to establish a case based on nothing.

After about 20 days, my interrogations began. For two to three days, they questioned me non-stop. For the final two days and nights, they would not allow me to sleep, taking turns questioning me. I was thoroughly exhausted and my mind often went completely blank as I constantly nodded off during their questioning. There was little I could do except withstand their physical beatings, tongue-lashings and stripping of my clothes and shoes.

They tortured me by locking me outside in the wintry cold. Eventually, they told me, "Your group has already been branded as cultic."

I asked them, "You say we are cultic, but have you any evidence of our illegal activity? Have we ever done anything to subvert national interests? What is your basis for labeling us as a cult? We are mainstream Christians. We serve God based on the Bible. Our disagreements with the Three-Self Patriotic Movement (TSPM) do not imply our opposition to the government. Our differences with the TSPM are based on matters of religious faith, not political issues. You say that the China Gospel Fellowship is an illegal organization, but the church is by nature an organization, based on the biblical model of church government, not a subversive movement."

My interrogators refused to address these issues, and simply said, "You people belong to the house churches. Whoever does not become part of the TSPM is a cult group. This is the definition from our superiors." Thus, my crime was determined.

After more than 40 days of imprisonment, they escorted more than ten of us from the Xinyang County 18 Mile Pingqiao Detention Prison onto a huge truck surrounded by Public Security vehicles. The truck we were on had labels pasted on all sides with slogans like "Resolute Attack on Cults," "Resolute Opposition toward Cults" and "Absolute Ban on Cults." With sirens blaring, we were paraded through the streets, and then brought to the huge hall at the town of the 13 Mile Bridge for public sentencing. All 14 of us, including two sisters, were chained together in a row as we stood in front of the chairman's podium.

JESUS - OUR HELP AND STRENGTH

The town hall was filled to capacity with mainly students. The chairman read out our "crimes" and announced the time span of corrective labor allocated to each of us. Four of us were sentenced to two years and the rest were given three years. A few days later, two more were sentenced, so there were 16 of us in all. As the sentences were given, some in the audience snickered, while others wept. As for us, we proudly stood with our chests out and our heads held high, because our consciences were clear of any form of guilt. We were hardly the type of "supposed cultists" they had accused us of being. In the evening, this event was broadcast on the local news network.

From that day onward, we began a new phase of life in the corrective facility. First of all, we were all ushered into the "Strict Scrutiny Group" to "undergo military training" to reform us. In the first month, no relatives were allowed to visit us. This applied only to Christians, however, as relatives of all other inmates were granted visits.

The corrective facility functioned on a much larger scale than the detention prison, so while we Christian brothers previously could not see each other for tens of days on end, we now could gather together more easily. We could care for one another's needs. For instance, if we noticed that a particular brother was malnourished, we would each save up part of our own very small allotted portion of food for the skinniest among us. One brother looked almost like a skeleton, so we accumulated some food to share with him. He consumed the equivalent of four persons' share of food, which gave us quite a fright. He shared with us that, at the detention prison, there were many days when he could not eat any food because there was a group of evil cellmates who would forcibly control his food supply. They would question him, "Do you believe in Jesus? If you do not believe, then you may eat. If you believe in Jesus, then don't eat. Let Jesus help you!" He replied: "I cannot forsake Jesus just because of food." Therefore, he ended up looking like a skeleton.

FORCED LABOR FOR FAITH IN CHRIST

Food supply in prison was already bad enough. Quantities were insufficient and food was cooked without salt or oil, and there was no meat and no vegetables. Some brothers had to forego their right to eat because they failed to complete their designated jobs for the day. Each person was allocated a stack of pig fur to separate the white from the black, a sorting job in preparation for the manufacture of leather goods. Others had to stitch flowers on a huge piece of cloth. We were told that these products were prepared for export, so quality control was especially tight. (The types of hard labor vary greatly, from assembling Christmas lights, to making bricks and digging in coal mines.) Failure to finish one's work would incur beatings, punishment and an empty stomach. Although our bodies were skinny, our spirits were fairly good. At least we had made it through the first phase. However, we knew that we still faced two to three years of intensive labor and we truly didn't know if we would survive it!

After a month of "strict scrutiny," they began to send us outdoors for labor. The ten brothers were assigned to different "Intensive Labor Teams." They were awakened at 5 o'clock in the morning and had to jog to the worksite. Lunch was at noon but they could not return to the prison until 9 o'clock at night. There were two kinds of jobs, both very strenuous: repairing roads and digging drains, and carrying soil and bricks. Everything was entirely work-oriented. Any mistake would earn you punches, kicks and even beatings with sticks. Everyone suffered much, but found no words to express their hardship and sorrow. Those who were physically weaker found the going especially difficult. In particular, Brother Wang had the worst ordeal of all because he had a snoring problem. After a hard day's work, who would want to listen to his snores during the short period of sleeping time allotted? He was beaten up countless times because of his snoring, so in order to avoid the beatings, he did not dare to sleep at night. Then the next day, because he was sleep deprived, he would doze off at work, hence earning another round of beating.

In order to keep Jesus' name from shame and glorify the Lord, all of us struggled to finish our assignments. At the worksite, there was no room for relaxation or casual talk. Only at night, after working long hours, could we secretly gather in small groups to encourage one another with God's Word. It was also during such sessions that the brothers would share with me the dumplings they had saved up. Since I was disabled, I could not join them at the worksite, so I remained within the "Strict Scrutiny Team," where we were never allowed to have a full meal, except when the top officials conducted their routine inspections. Only then would we have sufficient food and even some "welfare." Each Sunday after working hours, we were allowed to watch an hour of TV and about 200 of us would gather together.

After a period of time, we feared that we would gradually become estranged in our relationships with the Lord so we decided to use the weekly hour allocated for TV viewing to observe the Lord's Supper together. We would inform the brothers on the outside ahead of time, so that they could bring us some bread and grape juice during their visits. Through these special times of breaking bread together, we were able to renew our strength before our Lord. I recall one particular Sunday when the two brothers in charge of the meeting forgot where they had placed the bread. They started weeping bitterly over their blunder and made so much noise that even our fellow inmates watching TV turned their heads to see what was going on. The other brothers quickly reminded them to keep quiet. After that, we all sighed and said, "We Christians do not even have the right to weep."

When we first entered the corrective facility, we Christians were shunned by others, but over time, their attitudes changed. They could witness for themselves how Christians conscientiously endured the suffering, faithfully completed their tasks, dealt with integrity and treated others with courtesy. Even the supervising guards developed favorable opinions of Christians. Our actions and attitudes earned the accolades and respect of many. Whenever the officers had some critical matters on hand, they would entrust those tasks to the Christians. Subsequently, a few of our brothers were even promoted onto the "Supervision Team" who assisted the police in guarding the prisoners. People admired Christians, and the name of our Lord Jesus Christ was glorified. Gradually, the Gospel was also proclaimed within the facility.

In the afternoon of January 4, 1998, a policeman shouted out my name, asking me to quickly gather up my belongings. He said they had no need to sustain a good-for-nothing like me and they were immediately sending me home. Since all the inmates there had been purchased from the Public Security Bureau, everyone had to work. I could not believe my ears, so I asked him one more time if what he had said was true, to which he answered affirmatively. I then asked if any administrative procedures needed to be settled. He replied, "There is no need to do anything. Stop asking any more questions and get out of here. Don't ever come back here again!" By nightfall, I arrived at the home of brothers and sisters. I did not sleep that night, for I was anxious to know how the church was and they wanted to know about my experience in prison. The next day, before daybreak, I took a bus back to Tanghe.

JOY OVER THE MOON—REUNITED WITH FAMILY

Once I reached home, I searched everywhere for my wife and daughter. When I had left, of course, I knew where they were staying, but now I had no idea where they were hiding. I learned that before my wife had nursed our daughter for a full month, she had to pick her up and run because the Xinyang Public Security Bureau went to my hometown to find her. In fact, they had ransacked my Xinyang home and confiscated everything, including my worn leather jacket, before coming to Tanghe. Due to the urgency with which the informant warned my wife of the impending danger, she was afraid of unnecessarily implicating her host family. Therefore, that very night, fighting against the snow and cold winds, she waded through muddy roads to escape to another village. Because it was so cold, she was not able to fall asleep. Furthermore, she was afraid that Enbo would cry and disturb the neighbors, which might bring even more trouble. So she sat there in the cold all through the night, cuddling the baby.

During her month of confinement after childbirth, severe pain had developed in the vertebrae in her lower back. Thereafter, she went from house to house, hiding in each for only a few days. After my release, I went from family to family trying to find my wife and daughter and at the tenth home, I finally got information on her whereabouts.

A sister set off to bring my wife to where I was. When she heard that I was home, she was over the moon with joy and almost could not believe it was true. When my wife came home, I held our three-month-old daughter in my arms and repeatedly told her, "I am Daddy. I am home." Yet, her little eyes seemed frightened because she did not recognize me at all. After spending only a few days at home, I felt I must start my itinerant ministry again. My wife and Enbo also had to seek alternative dwelling. Because she had to travel so much, my daughter developed a form of phobia whereby noises would cause her entire little body to shudder. It was only after a full year that such symptoms began to recede.

KIDNAPPED BY EASTERN LIGHTNING CULT

CHAPTER V

April 16, 2002 is a day that I shall never forget. On that day, 34 of our co-workers were kidnapped by the evil cult Eastern Lightning. I was one of those victims involved. This was a carefully designed plot. Events started unfolding back in April of 2001. In Pingdingshan of Henan province, a house church preacher named Ai Yanling informed Brother Yang, a prominent leader in her church, that she knew a sister whose relative was a staff worker with the Haggai Institute in Singapore. This sister had business dealings in Guangzhou and Beijing. She had expressed her desire to meet with house church leaders because she wished to sponsor suitable candidates to enroll in the Haggai Institute. Brother Yang subsequently met with Mr. Lian, the self-proclaimed staff worker with the Haggai Institute, and his daughter. During the conversation, father and daughter said they were originally from this region, and now wished to do something for the church in their hometown. They had thought about sponsoring those who had a desire to study at the Haggai Institute in Singapore. They then asked Brother Yang to submit his biographical information, along with his phone number, photograph and a copy of his identity card to Mr. Lian, who would then relay the information to the Institute for consideration. After Brother Yang had submitted the necessary documents, they told him that signatures and letters of recommendation from his co-workers in leadership were also necessary. Otherwise, the Institute would not accept his application. They then said they were willing to meet with and converse with Brother Yang's church leaders.

When Brother Yang found his leader, Old Brother Shen,

he asked Shen to write him a letter of recommendation and also invited Shen to meet with Mr. Lian and his daughter. During the meeting, Brother Shen mentioned that the house churches lacked formal theological training, needed to strengthen biblical foundations, and were constantly harassed by cult groups. Shen then asked Mr. Lian to please assist the house churches so that more people would have the opportunity to receive training. Mr. Lian replied, "I am a businessman. My original intention was just to visit my hometown and mind my own business, but God disciplined me by causing a recurrence of an ailment from which I was already completely healed in my youth. I prayed to God and confessed my sins to Him. My ailment was immediately healed, and I realize I have no choice but to submit to God's will and help you out." He promised Brother Shen that he would petition the Institute's administrators to accept more students, and asked Brother Shen and his co-workers to submit their biographical information to him. After that, an entire year went by without further communication.

In March 2003, Mr. Lian suddenly called by phone and said, "The Institute has given the matter much thought, and eventually decided that my daughter and I will lead the Institute's principal, Mr. Yu, and the sister in charge of finances to pay a visit so that they may better understand the actual circumstances at Pingdingshan." The party arrived in Yingyang county in Henan province at the home of Mr. Lian's older sister where discussions were held. During the meeting, they explained that there had been no communication for the past year because the Institute's administration was struggling over whether or not to enroll students from Mainland China. Mr. Lian and his daughter had worked feverishly to seek approval, which has culminated in the principal's visit. After about two hours, we left Yingyang county but they said that a final decision had yet to be made.

A few weeks later, Mr. Lian called again and asked to meet with a few co-workers. He also presented us with a brief history of the Haggai Institute so that we may better understand this Institute's operations. He said that the Institute had given approval, but was worried that these prospective students would not get their passports done in time to make the trip to Singapore. Therefore, the administration was willing to introduce us to six families in China through which the Haggai Institute was conducting training. We objected to their proposal, saying, "We are all very busy. In the villages, it is just about time for the wheat harvest and we are unable to immediately enroll in this training program. Moreover, our learning at the Haggai Institute is not something that can be accomplished within six months to a year. Even if we were to enroll immediately, not all of us could go at once. At the most, we can send two co-workers each year. With regard to participation in training conducted in China, let's talk about it some other time." Still, their persistence and insistence was hard to resist, so we told them that we only had a window of two weeks. We all agreed to this in haste without more extensive consideration. Our minds were then solely preoccupied with getting ourselves better equipped with knowledge of the truth. Little did we know that we would soon be walking into their trap. Only later did we realize that the two women from Pingdingshan were the undercover agents of the Eastern Lightning cult.

DESTRUCTIVE DECEPTION

On April 15, 34 of our co-workers set off from different locations and reported at the six designated venues (i.e., Shanghai, Qingdao, Haerbin, Hebei, Xian and Hubei). On April 16, a few co-workers and I arrived from Zhengzhou, Henan province to Shanghai. They transported us in a vehicle to a home located in the city. Not long after we sat down, an elderly person outside the house kept monitoring us through the window. They told us that this man was a member of the residents' committee who was fond of minding other people's business. Then, the principal appeared troubled as he hurriedly came over and told us, "Things are not going to well. A brother from headquarters in Shanghai has warned me of an impending wave of major persecution directed at the church. They said the government will begin to attack the house churches. Our situation is very dangerous, so let us disperse immediately." Thus, they separated the four of us brothers. Four others belonging to the "Head-covering sect" were also forced to split into two groups. (In actual fact, they were working with the Eastern Lightning.) In two separate vehicles, we were transported to a home on the outskirts of Shanghai. Later on, we realized that the 34 of us had been distributed to 17 different families to "undergo training," for truly, they intended to brainwash us.

On April 17, "classes" officially commenced with six teachers instructing us four students, although in reality, two of the students were with them.

On the second day of class, I said to the teacher surnamed Chen, "What you are talking about sounds so much like what Eastern Lightning advocates proclaim."

"The Eastern Lightning advocates talk about the Bible, and so do we," he explained patiently. "It is inevitable that there will be areas of commonality."

Since we were under the assumption that these were instructors from the Haggai Institute in Singapore, we let our guard down. Furthermore, we noticed that they demonstrated much love, gentleness, humility and fervency in their service. Thus, we were even less prudent.

On the night of April 18, everyone had gone to other parts of the house when a lady came into my room and chatted with me. She had quite a story to tell. She said that she was an orphan whose father had left for Singapore prior to the Cultural Revolution. Once the Revolution started, he could no longer return to China, so he started another family in Singapore. Her mother and she relied on each other for survival, but after her university graduation, her mother passed away. She then went to Singapore to be with her father. Not long after her arrival, her father and stepmother perished in an airline accident and she was left all alone. However, she had a huge inheritance that she didn't have to share with anyone since she had no siblings. Subsequently, she married a self-proclaimed Christian. When her husband went to the United States for business, he fell in love with another woman, so again she was left alone.

Without any relatives in China, she felt very lonely and asked if I would be her older brother. After I listened to her tragedy, I comforted her with the words of Scripture, but she grabbed my arm with both her hands. This startled me and I pulled away from her.

She quickly left my room as I sat thinking to myself, "Why are foreign Chinese so open?" The next day, I was alone in my room once again and this lady came in and sat in front of me, her eyes looking straight into mine. I instantly realized that something was amiss, and told her, "You must seek to influence your husband through Christ's love so that he may repent. You must never lose rational control and fall into the devil's schemes during times of loneliness." She was stunned by my words, and turned and rushed out of the room.

Two days later, the principal requested that I write a letter comforting those who were undergoing training at the various venues, reminding them to be obedient, not move around on their own without permission, and to maintain cordial relations with those of the Head-covering sect. I did not yet suspect anything and did not realize that this was a scheme, so I proceeded to write the letter. Subsequently, I also completed two assignments concerning how to change the practices of the Head-covering sect. Only later did I discover that they scanned my letter into a computer, made changes to the contents based on my handwriting, and then distributed the altered version to various places. How devious of them!

For the first 20 days or so, two to three "teachers" would talk about the Old Testament and its history. No major problems surfaced. However, about a week later, Old Brother Shen told me secretly in the lavatory, "I'm afraid these people belong to the Eastern Lightning cult. Those two from the Head-covering sect are working with them and I wonder why no females accompany them, while ladies serve us constantly? Moreover, I have noticed that that one particular woman's behavior is immoral. She's a temptress. You must be extra careful." After we left the lavatory, Old Brother Shen added, "We in the Chinese house churches have our rules. We maintain socially acceptable distance between males and females. Those of the opposite sex must never get too close to one another."

The lady surnamed Lian heard these words and started crying. The instructors came over to us and said, "Your comments were too harsh. Sister Lian is still single and you have shamed her. Foreign Chinese are relatively more open in their ways." After this conversation and after she had dried her tears, Sister Lian proceeded to give Old Brother Shen a head massage. (This is because Brother Shen had an ailment concerning blood vessels to his brain.) I thought to myself, "How are these people so loving and patient?"

I found an opportune moment and I asked those from the Head-covering sect, "How long have you known these people?" They replied, "For a couple of years. We've had constant contact with their churches." Once again, I let my guard down and was not as discerning and careful as I should have been.

On April 29, they said that it was almost time to celebrate Labor Day on May 1, when workers receive a long vacation. The relatives of this host family would soon return, so we had to disperse ourselves for a few days. Hence, at around 9 o'clock that night, a vehicle came and took away Old Brother Shen along with two of the teachers and a young lady. A member of the Head-covering sect and I remained behind to continue studying the Scriptures.

On May 4, when they resumed their teaching, it was now clearly contrary to scriptural truth. I rebutted with a few words of my own and decided not to listen to their lectures any longer. I also decided to fast for two to three days, going completely without food.

PREPARED TO DIE FOR MY FAITH

On May 5, they made a stunning declaration and openly declared, "We proclaim the message of Eastern Lightning." The moment I heard that, I exploded and furiously reprimanded them, "You are a group of gangsters, robbers of the church, false-christs, anti-christs, serpents draped in human skin, the filth of society! I will never forego my correct beliefs and follow your ridiculous teachings!" I further emphasized to them my stance, saying, "I won't listen, I won't watch, I won't think, I won't debate and I won't believe." I wanted them to give up any hope of converting me. I reminded them that all their tactics would be in vain.

I also realized that I was in a very dangerous situation and had no way of escaping, as I was under guard. I had no idea how they were going to deal with me but I had thoughts of the four Christians from my hometown who had been captured by the Eastern Lightning and had their arms and legs fractured and their mouths slit and their ears cut off. I wondered if I might be in for a similar fate. Furthermore, I had opposed the Eastern Lightning for many years by making known their evil deeds. I had even rescued some who had been bewitched by their lies. I thought they must hate me very much. So revenge was to be expected. I was prepared to be a Christian martyr. Despite using all the means they could think of, I stood by my policy of "Five Won'ts—won't listen, watch, think, debate, or believe." When they had run out of ideas, they daily assaulted me with verbal scoldings, calling me a Pharisee, a crucifier of Jesus, an opponent of God, and threatened me with punishment, curses and destruction.

The member of the Head-covering sect kept yelling all through the night as he tried to sleep. The next day, he told me. "Last night, I saw a vision. I heard the voice of angels, saying, 'God has already come. Hurry and believe. Do not resist. Otherwise, you will perish.'"

"Last night, I too had a dream," I told him. "Someone told me that all this is untrue. It is the lie of false prophets and the trickery of the devil." I went on to tell him, "Even if I never had that dream, I still will not believe your pseudo-truths."

Around May 7, they told me, "Since you refuse to accept our message, we are sending you home. Tonight, we will allow you to meet with the co-workers. Tomorrow, we will let you go." At 9:00 pm, a group of people dragged me into a vehicle. After a convoluted journey, I arrived at another home, where I was interned. It was a small, two-story building. I was locked in a room where the doors were firmly secured with ropes from the outside. The window panes were covered over with green paint in order that no light could shine through. There were guards both inside and outside my room and I lay on my bed, neither listening to nor looking at them. Each day they would preach to me and scold me. They never stopped twisting the Scriptures in defiance of true biblical teaching. In between, they would play CDs containing their songs. During the day, I withstood their assault but during the night, I had difficulty sleeping because I neither ate nor drank (out of fear that they would drug me as they were known to often do). My scalp felt like it was rotting. In body, spirit and soul, I was being tortured.

One morning, they suddenly declared that they were all going outside to discuss some matters. The member of the

Head-covering sect also left. I thought to myself: "Today may be my vacation. Perhaps I can get a day of rest without any of their psychological torture." Not long after, a lady came in, secured all three doors to the room and sat down in front of me. She was mumbling something as she made advances toward me. I was then lying down in bed, so she forcefully embraced me and I moved my head from side to side to avoid her efforts to kiss me while she uttered shameless words. I tried my best to resist while praying unceasingly and earnestly to the Lord that He would deliver me from temptation. In the end, I had no choice but to sit up and yell, "I am a Christian! I am a married man!" She was not able to get through my defenses and so she left.

ESCAPE FROM EVIL CULT

During the final week, because I started hitting the windows and repeatedly shouted for help, they stopped preaching to me. I noticed that there was a different look on all their faces and they looked very troubled. It seemed as if something serious had occurred. On the afternoon of June 3, I was escorted into a vehicle and taken to the Shanghai train station. Thank God, I had finally been released! In all, I was interned for a full 50 days. I had finally escaped from the clutches of the evil one; however, my body had been tortured beyond human form. My appearance was ghastly, and my bony frame looked like a twig.

Upon my return, I learned that my family members had long known about our kidnapping. A sister from the Northeast had managed to escape and she had informed the various churches, where brothers and sisters prayed fervently for us. Two other brothers also struggled with their captors and escaped. Because the situation was so serious, they even reported the matter to the Public Security Bureau, the police. They were scouring the countryside and any known Eastern Lighting location and finally, under extreme pressure from the police, the Eastern Lightning was forced to release us. If not for this turn in events, I don't know whether or not I would still be alive, or when I would have been able to escape from their clutches.

In this instance, our brothers and sisters petitioned the authorities without much hindrance. Within three days, the Public Security Bureau took up the case and mobilized their police from different regions in a large-scale operation to hunt down the culprits. Our brothers and sisters played their part by actively locating Eastern Lightning strongholds. The Eastern Lightning cultists never expected that house church Christians would make a police report, because they knew that the house churches were considered illegal and, in fact, were being pursued by these same forces. They assumed that house church Christians would never seek help from the authorities, no matter how much suffering they had to undergo. And it was true that within our church ranks, members had been divided as to whether or not to make the police report. Some had been afraid that doing so not only would not rescue the kidnapped, but would actually further jeopardize those making the report. We were pleasantly surprised at how smoothly our case was processed. It exceeded all our expectations. Never before had the Public Security Bureau acted so swiftly. Little did we expect that the Public Security officials would regard us house church Christians as citizens.

On June 20, we organized an open forum exposing the evil ways of the Eastern Lightning. Each of those kidnapped shared their experiences. We related how the Eastern Lightning used despicable tactics such as deception, deceit, financial enticement, sexual temptation, drugs, pretense, rage, intimidation, isolation, mind control and disruption of family life. Through this forum, everyone realized that our previous understanding of the Eastern Lightning was insufficient. We lacked prudence, and our concept of public law was too superficial and it had resulted in a major setback for our church. Nonetheless, human folly could still accomplish God's good purposes and God's power is revealed through human weakness.

Through this series of trials, each one of us was severely tested with regard to our knowledge of our Lord Jesus Christ, our steadfastness with respect to biblical truth, our trust in God, and also our moral integrity. Through this fiery trial, we had matured. We realized our inadequacies before the Lord and our frivolous disregard toward the potential threat of the Eastern Lightning. We had not shown enough understanding and concern for those who had departed from the way of truth. Neither did we realize that proponents of Eastern Lightning teachings would stoop to such depths of depravity. Through prayer and sharing, we diminished our misunderstandings and strengthened our fellowship. Our faith was more firmly established as we more clearly recognized our common goal. Together, we must fight the good fight for the truth.

UNDERGROUND TRAINING CENTER

This underground training center continues in use today at a very secret location. It took 18 months of digging with hand tools to carve out this main meeting room where 60 pastors in training and Bible students study 16 hours a day, 7 days a week for 30 days at a time. Simple plastic stools are the only furniture they can afford.

The access tunnel is narrow and there are two additional small areas carved out to house the women and men separately. There is a small cove that serves as a bathroom with buckets that are carried up, through the tunnel and emptied every day. There is no provision for washing and every two weeks, if conditions allow, they slip up above to quickly clean up.

In the rainy season, there is often water lying on the floor but training continues. It is damp and dark and the air becomes foul. But nothing dampens the enthusiasm of these lovers of the Word of God as they soak up all their teachers can pour into them during the intensive 30-day period of study.

Over the past 15 years, although 3,000 pastors and believers in this region have been arrested, this training center has continued to safely func-

tion and over 1,000 pastors and Christian workers have received training at this location alone.

WorldServe provided for the costs of electrical power to be run down and prior to that, they only had candles and lanterns. In other locations WorldServe has been able to provide benches and chairs. The needs are so great; we just do what we can to help. Even simple stools or benches are greatly appreciated.

Although 3,000 pastors and believers in this region have been arrested, this training center continues

The term "underground church" has evolved over many years but had its beginning when all churches in China were forcibly closed and the only way believers could meet together was in secret, in the dark of night, and in the fields and forests. Even during the intense persecution of the Cultural Revolution (1966-1976) small groups of believers continued to meet. Before long, the need for security and total secrecy led believers to dig secret rooms, physically located under the surface of the ground or in caves.

Not all locations are literally underground but all are in secret locations, usually consisting of just one meeting room, where men and women, young and old, dedicate themselves to be equipped for ministry.

'05 5 5

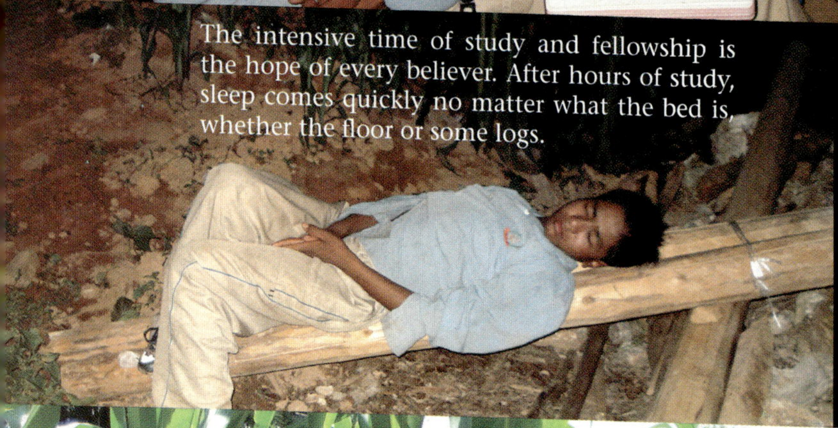

The intensive time of study and fellowship is the hope of every believer. After hours of study, sleep comes quickly no matter what the bed is, whether the floor or some logs.

Upon completing their training, usually teams of two single individuals or couples are sent out to minister, seeking to win friends and people to Christ everywhere they go.

The underground church in China is known for great dedication in outreach, exuberant worship and great fervor in prayer that shakes the gates of heaven. The average size house church may be around 50 believers but in rural areas, the numbers commonly reach 200-300 and more. Large meetings of 1,000 and more also take place and on special occasions, even within the last year, gatherings of 8,000 – 10,000 believers have taken place in the countryside.

Most house churches in China today are in fact homes and most actual underground facilities are used more for training. If it were not for "host" families, the dedicated families who open up their homes to hold church services, times of prayer, worship and training, there would be no house church in China. The host families risk arrest and the confiscation of all their belongings but tens of thousands of families faithfully offer up all they have for the cause of Christ. Many have lost all their possessions multiple times but still they continue to "host" the church.

One of the great needs is to assist the "host" families as all are poor and can only share what they have with those being housed by them. Simple assistance for vegetables and more protein is greatly needed as many survive primarily on noodles, congee (rice broth) and mantou (a steamed white bread).

Incredibly, the "underground" church is often found outside, in plain sight, both day and night. This is possible as local officials may be believers, or they may have so many relatives who are believers that they look the other way. In some cases, the numbers of believers in a specific locality are so great that they meet regardless of the threats and pressure. The pastors laugh as they say, "They can't arrest us all."

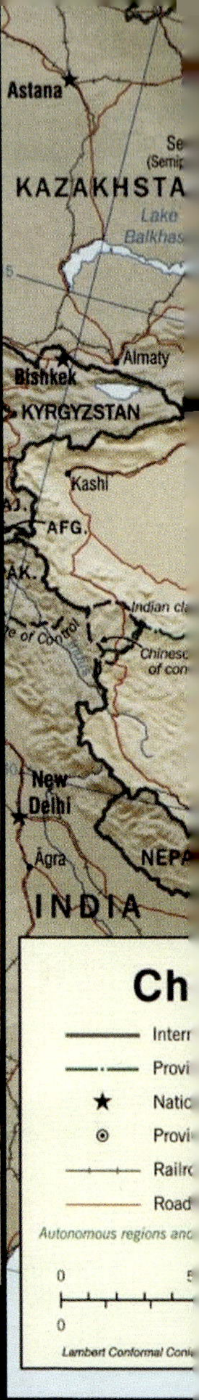

The Church in China has been scattered by persecution just as the early church was scattered by persecution. This has only fuelled the growth of the church. As pastors and evangelists in China have had to run from village to village and province to province, "Those who had been scattered preached the word wherever they went." Acts 8:4

Today, the Gospel has penetrated every city and province in China and the result has been the greatest turning to Christ in history. The underground church continues to grow in size and stature and today is estimated to number some 80 million believers.

To describe the locations as "simple" would greatly understate the deplorable conditions under which much of the underground church must meet. However, the absolutely packed rooms, often overflowing outside, and the enthusiastic worship, prayer and powerful preaching cause the surroundings to fade into oblivion as these dedicated followers of Christ turn their eyes to Jesus, seeing nothing else.

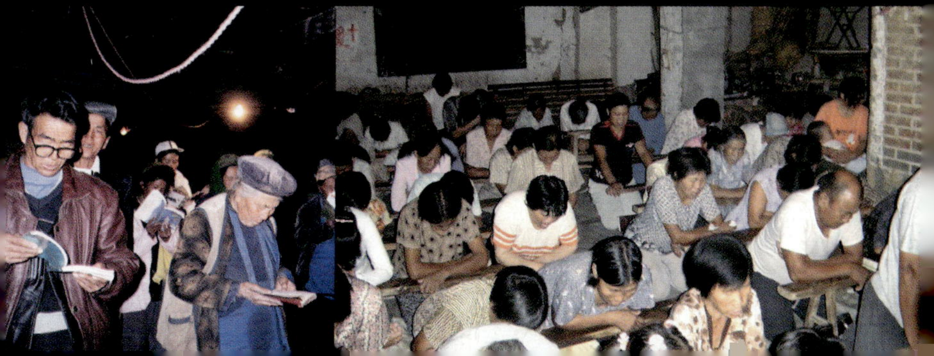

Often the floor is dirt but always swept clean and there the believers kneel to pray, sit by the hour, sleep and have their simple meals. As many must travel great distances, the "host" family always does what it can to

welcome the weary traveler, provide a bucket for washing and a simple meal, even if it is mostly broth.

As most of the house church is rural, there are no heating systems and even in the dead of winter, the believers continue to meet and typically are not dressed well enough for the weather. The winter is an especially difficult time for all, as to travel and meet in the bitter cold is difficult. But gather they do, with rosy cheeks, cold hands and warm hearts to worship the Lord.

China, with its vast size and varied geographic makeup, contains virtually every land type and weather condition found anywhere in the world. This presents a great challenge to the church planters as they travel tens of hours to reach their area of ministry and then often must walk 10-15 miles per day to reach the isolated communities. They traverse steep mountain trails; climb to high plateaus and cross inhospitable deserts. They endure the heat of summer and harsh winters all with the burning desire to win their countrymen for Christ.

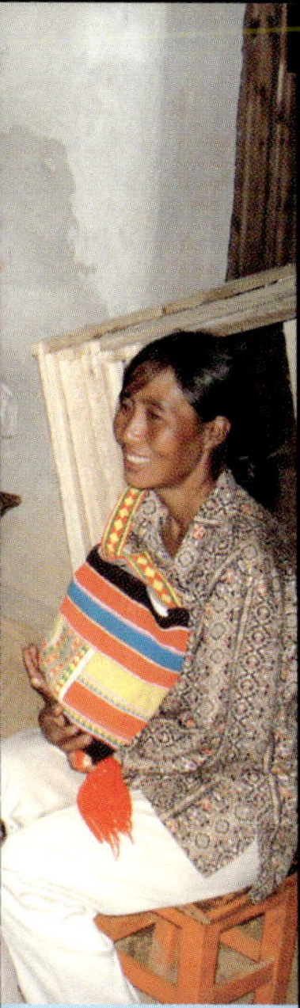

In the last five years, there has been a concerted effort by the underground church of China to reach the most remote parts of the country as well as to reach out to the large numbers of ethnic minorities. Although still within the boundaries of China, the evangelists and church planters must seek to understand the very different cultures they encounter, with unfamiliar dress, food, local customs and language. This they do with great diligence in order to more effectively communicate the Gospel.

The greatest migration in history is taking place that will ultimately see 300 million people migrate from their rural surroundings to urban areas according to experts. The underground church in China is struggling to embrace this great move and is establishing churches in every major city in the country. As well, every university in the country has young people from the underground church attending to further their education, but more importantly, to reach their fellow students for Christ. The constraints for the underground church are many but one of the major difficulties they face is to cover the cost to place a team of church planters in a city. The cost is easily 4-5 times what it is to reach rural areas and without assistance from believers outside China, it would be nearly impossible for the underground church to overcome this barrier

> **The underground church is establishing churches in every major city in the country**

on its own. WorldServe is financially assisting not just the rural church planters but increasingly enabling teams of urban church planters to have the financial means to effectively minister in the cities of China.

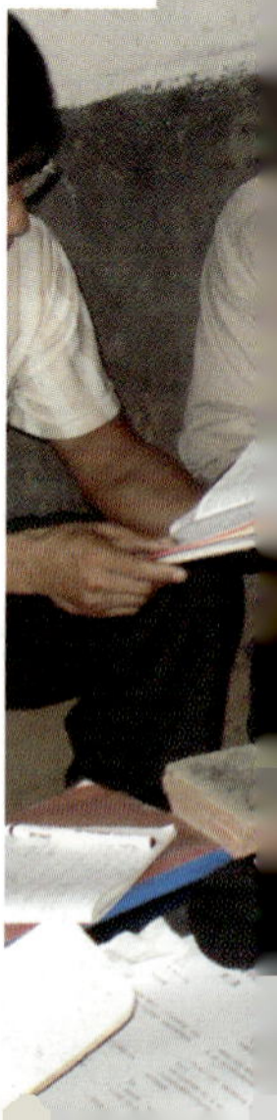

Another barrier is the sophistication of the city folk compared to those who have come from the village. But God is greatly using the dedicated church planters and young students and evangelists to win and disciple thousands of city dwellers. In the cities, the underground church primarily meets in the "host" family's apartment or rented facilities and sometimes even in the park.

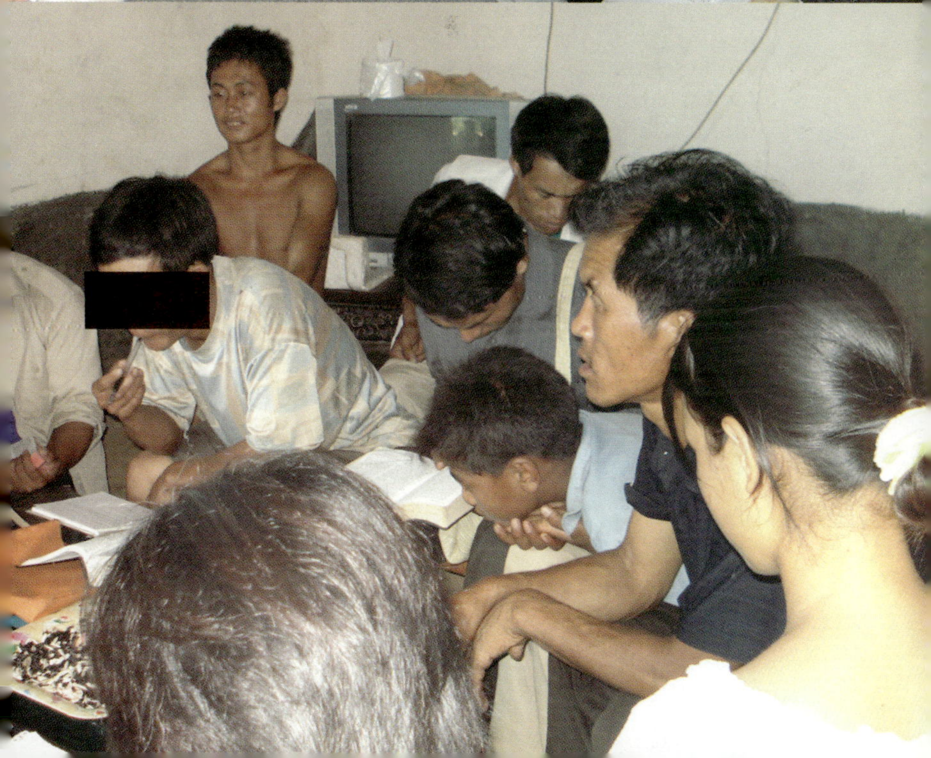

THE MOST TREASURED POSESSION FOR EVERY BELIEVER IN CHINA

GOD'S PRECIOUS WORD

During the Cultural Revolution, virtually all the Bibles in China were destroyed. Many pastors, for the entire 10 year period, never set their eyes on a single copy of God's Word. When it was learned that someone had a Bible in a neighboring village, there would be a stream of people traveling to go and try to get a glimpse of the precious Bible. Many gave their lives to protect the hiding place of a Bible. Many more went to prison. Many gave years of their lives to hand copy the entire Bible to give to others.

Every precious verse and chapter and book in a believers' possession was committed to memory or copied and passed along. No church in the world has a greater love for the Word of God than the underground church in China! The believers understand the value and dynamic, life-changing power in the Word. Only by going to the Word in prayer and hiding God's Word in their hearts have the believers been able to withstand the suffering, the persecution, the beatings and imprisonment. Only by grounding the work of the Spirit of God on the Word of God has the remarkable revival been able to be sustained and sweep tens of millions into the Kingdom of God.

Often in the dark of night, only after a long day's work can a believer spend time in the Word by flash-light or candle light. Young or old, all treasure the Bible above all else. When

they don't have enough Bibles to go around (which is a constant condition in China) they share with one another and copy what they can and pass it on. WorldServe since 1980, has been providing the Word of God for the underground church in China and our prayer and desire is to provide at least 1 million Bibles each year. The printing and distribution all takes place in China and the only limitation at this time is the finances. It costs $2.50 to print and put a Bible into the hands of a pastor or new believer. Even combining all the work of all the great agencies that are providing Bibles, there remains a staggering 30 to 50 million believers who still do not own a Bible. All of us together can't even keep up with the new believers each year, let alone, supply the believers from years past. We do what we can and the church in China continues to pray for the Lord to supply and they continue to memorize and copy large portions of Scripture.

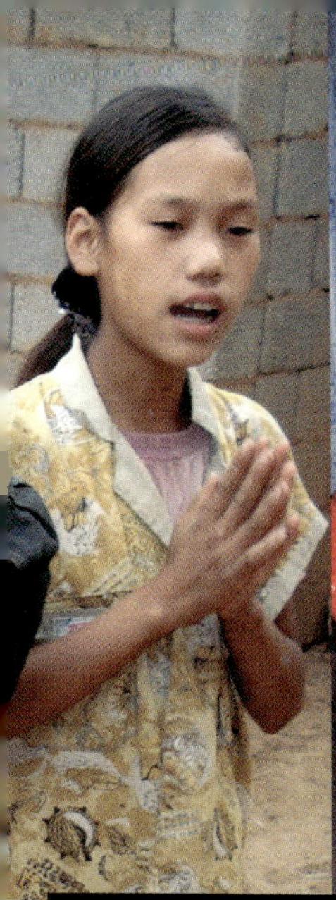

One of the great untold stories of the underground church in China is the ministry to children. Although technically there is a Chinese law allowing the religious education of minors, in reality, it is not permissible for the underground church to do so. Every year, countless numbers of Christian workers who work with children, along with Sunday School teachers, are arrested for ministering with children. However, neither pressure nor persecution will stop the underground church from sharing Christ with the children of China.

Part 2

ENVISIONING THE FUTURE

IN AN ERA OF REFORMS

CHAPTER VI

I was born during the era of Mao Zedong, an era marked by combative struggles. In Mao's own words: "There is unlimited joy in battling against the heavens, against the earth and against fellow human beings." These struggles were targeted at landowners, wealthy farmers, anti-revolutionaries, evildoers, rightists, all religious affiliates and all Christians. Several million people were labeled as "evil" and forced to squat in cowsheds, put on tall hats to be humiliated, be subjected to beatings and scoldings, and finally trampled upon in such a way that they never again regained their former dignity. Wave upon wave of such political movements left behind a culture that was combative and filled with hatred. Even father and son would turn against one another. No one was exempt from impending danger. One can only imagine how Christians survived those perilous times.

The era of Deng Xiaoping, on the other hand, was marked by reform and openness. Deng disliked struggles, and used slogans like "No Disputes," "White Cat, Black Cat," "One Country, Two Systems," "Development is Solid Truth," and so forth. He thereby did away with many unreasonable political policies such as "Huge Pot of Rice," "Ideology of Equal Distribution," and "Slice with One Knife." We moved from a planned economy toward a market economy. Such reforms were a giant step forward for China. Millions upon millions of people left their hometowns and migrated to the cities to do business or to seek employment. There was tremendous freedom for mobility. It was amidst this change in climate that the church began to turn from looking inward to focusing outward.

The era of Jiang Zemin has been hailed as the third generation of leadership in Communist China. Jiang advocated the theory of "Three Representations," which immediately became so important that it inundated the daily newspapers, airwaves, and TV stations. When political leaders hosted foreign emissaries, this was a mandatory topic for discussion. This "Three Representations" theory became widely credited with every sort of progress, be it the development of a small region, the prosperity of a certain market, the advancement of new scientific methodologies, the screening of a new movie, the visit of a government official, or the rescue operations of the police force. The Chinese Communist Party began to proclaim the slogan: "Keep up with the Times; Reform and Renew."

In a 2002 article titled "China and the World," a French author wrote: "China has become the stage on which the drama of reform is being performed with much pomp and vigor. This reformation has come about faster than predicted." He added, "Currently, China is still undergoing social, political and cultural reforms."

One can easily discern from these observations that the Chinese people have already opened the curtains to a new era of change. I believe that further political reform is a certainty. For a country to become great, she must make progress toward civilization, which entails the following two basic criteria:

1. socio-political humanitarianism as evidenced by a cultural spirit of benevolence; and
2. socio-political rationalization through reason and science.

The direction and outlet for modern China is the cultural pursuit of objectivity and truthfulness. Not only is this the trend of the times but also the desire of the people. We trust that history will not go into reverse. We hope and pray that someday we will see a civilized, free and open China where the disruption and persecution of Christians and their gatherings will be a thing of the past. The question is: How will today's "house church" face these new circumstances? What form will she take? If the situation does, indeed, slacken in terms of governmental control, will she have to register? Will she register according to geographical location? What will that registration look like? What will her responsibility toward society be? These are questions that demand serious consideration. Church and state are separate, but Christians cannot ignore politics because the two are intimately intertwined. For all these years, Christians have been hesitant to comment too extensively on this sensitive issue of politics for fear of being swept into this complicated whirlpool. With each wave of political upheaval, Chinese Christians have tended to adopt an attitude of withdrawal. This has resulted in a passive church.

I believe that if the government assumes an open attitude, it will recognize the legality of the house churches, and Christians must be ready to reciprocate. It is not impossible to envision the house churches and the Chinese government as equal partners in dialogue. We know what our stance and responsibility is: Christians are to be salt and light in the world, ready to purify the world through the Lord's love, justice and holiness. We are to be law-abiding, reprimanding sinful behavior while opposing corruption and decadence. However, we must also remember that we must not get entangled in political matters. We need to maintain our allegiance to biblical principles while gradually engaging our immediate circumstances with flexibility, wisdom and prudence.

SERVANT LEADERS BORN IN THE FIRE OF PERSECUTION

The house churches grew amidst adverse extenuating circumstances. During the Cultural Revolution, most who believed in Jesus were either ill or uncultured or both. Even the revival of the 1980s started predominantly from the farming communities, and those who were raised up as leaders were likewise of lower social and cultural standards. However, the ones used by God possessed a heart lovingly devoted to the Lord. They willingly dedicated their lives for the Lord's use and through hard work, evangelism, healings, exorcisms, deeds of love and fervent persuasion, they established churches one after another. Thus, they also earned the respect of the brethren, and unknowingly, these "unschooled, ordinary men" became the leaders of their respective local churches.

As church congregations grew in number and areas of influence increased in size, some became leaders in charge of churches spanning several tens of counties. Since they had never been through formal theological training, and their spiritual gifts and knowledge were incomplete, these leaders withstood tremendous pressure. In the face of missions ministries, pastoral duties, polemics against cults, church management, cooperation among co-workers, human relations, children's education and family life, many leaders felt that they were not up to the task. Yet, they were caught in a dilemma: there was nowhere to move beyond these responsibilities, and it was impossible to just step down and leave. Like an aged ox dragging a broken-down cart, these leaders trotted along their wobbly ways, constantly struggling with discouragement, fatigue, personal weaknesses and a lack of ability. Some were even overcome by Satan as they succumbed to temptations.

It is evident that church leaders urgently need to be better equipped for their tasks so as to improve on the quality and character of the church as a whole. The Bible has much to teach us in this respect, complete with many distinct role models we should emulate, as well as negative examples we ought to avoid. When a good leader arises, he will bring great blessing and revival to his country, his people and his church. On the contrary, a poor leader brings down curses from above, and reaps turmoil, poverty and desecration. Even as leaders of this world must come equipped with certain credentials, how much more spiritual leaders of the church must possess even higher standards of character.

In 1 Timothy 3, the apostle Paul wrote about the credentials of spiritual leadership: a good reputation with outsiders, above reproach, monogamous and a worthy example for others to imitate. In character, he must be gentle and loving, not greedy for money or power. At home, he must manage his household well and instruct his children. In terms of spirituality, he must constantly pursue maturity while avoiding pride and impatience. A leader must be clear about God's calling and regularly spend time in devotion and prayer so as to maintain a fervent heart. Furthermore, he must be ever ready to sacrifice, withstand pressure, carry himself appropriately, be courageous in leadership, steadfast in principle, defending the truth and faithfully keeping watch on behalf of the flock as he attempts to fill any gaps in the church.

In terms of church vision, a spiritual leader must have

clear direction, distribute work reasonably, and work well with a team. It is his responsibility to stir up the spiritual climate of the church so that the brothers and sisters there will each possess a heart of reverence, service and hunger for God, thereby boosting church morale and unity as church members dedicate themselves to God, each other and the church's mission. Only under the guidance of the Holy Spirit can the church innovatively develop spiritual ministries.

Church leadership is not equivalent to secular leadership because it does not resort to power and politics, but emulates our Lord Jesus Christ in willingness to sacrifice oneself in humble service as slaves loved by God. From church history, we can identify a few types of leaders: those who use power to oppress, those who lead by punishment, those who lure followers with benefits, those who attract others with their wisdom, and those who earnestly lead by being servants. Our Lord Jesus said:

> *You know that the rulers of the Gentiles lord it over them, and their high officials exercise authority over them. Not so with you. Instead, whoever wants to become great among you must be your servant, and whoever wants to be first must be your slave—just as the Son of Man did not come to be served, but to serve, and to give his life as a ransom for many.*
>
> ***Matthew 20:25-28***

PRISON LEADS TO UNITY

In spring of 1998, there were major developments in the house churches throughout China. Simultaneously, persecution was rampant and the Eastern Lightning cult continued to disrupt our ministries. These common threats compelled brothers and sisters to huddle together in unison to combat this truly heretical cult group.

Fangcheng church was the closest among all our affiliated churches. Their leader Brother Zhang and the leader of the Tanghe church, Uncle Feng, had become acquainted in 1975, a year when the church in China saw great persecution. Many brothers and sisters were imprisoned, publicly insulted, paraded and even labeled as counter-revolutionaries. Uncle Feng was sentenced to a five-year jail term and was sent to the corrective facility in Nanyang. Not long after, due to an excess of workers, some inmates, including Uncle Feng, were transferred to the Xihua corrective facility in Henan province. By then, Uncle Feng had already become friends with a few brothers in Nanyang, and they were fearful at this imposed separation from one another.

Uncle Feng worried, "I'm not sure I will survive in a new place so far away from home where I have no acquaintances."

One brother tried to encourage him, "I've heard people say that there is a Brother Zhang Rongliang in the Xihua corrective facility at Fangcheng. You should seek him out so you could help one another."

Uncle Feng replied, "In a facility covering tens of acres, how can I possibly find him? Moreover, there isn't even an inch of freedom in that place. No freedom to casually talk or walk."

But everyone agreed, "There is no other way. All you can do is pray and entrust everything to the Lord. And we will pray, too."

Later, 600 convicts were transferred together to the Xihua facility. Upon arrival, the supervising officers allocated each person a lodging place, distributing the new inmates among the existing prisoners. This process dragged on until nightfall. Toward the end, one officer pointed at Uncle Feng and said, "We still have one old fellow over here unallocated." "What is your crime?" an officer asked Uncle Feng. Uncle Feng answered, "Religious counter-revolutionism." That officer then shouted out, "Zhang Rongliang, this man is allocated to your section. He will stay with you tonight."

Thus, Uncle Feng and Brother Zhang amazingly got acquainted with one another by God's grace. A few days later, Uncle Feng was transferred to the apple plantation while Brother Zhang remained to continue feeding the pigs. Henceforth, any relatives visiting one would also proceed to visit the other and share any gifts of food or clothing. Over time, intimate bonds of fellowship in the Lord were forged.

Five years of corrective labor established a strong friendship between these two men, and also between the churches at

Tanghe and Fangcheng. After 1990, due to differences in opinion, these ties were disrupted. Not until the fall of 1996 did we begin to realize the importance of ecclesiastical unity (between the major groups). Thus, brotherly bonds were renewed and we sought to broaden our network of fellowship. In November of 1998, a few house churches gathered in Northern China and drafted a "Faith Declaration" as the foundation for ecclesiastical unity. Over the years, we got to know one another better through fellowship. We shared our knowledge, broadened our perspectives and renewed our visions for ministry. We worked together in combating heresy and also learned valuable spiritual lessons while supplementing one another's strengths and weaknesses.

DENOMINATIONALISM DRIVING A WEDGE BETWEEN HOUSE CHURCH MOVEMENTS

Prior to the current series of reforms, secular Chinese people in their tunnel vision have tended to label Christianity as a Western religion, which in turn spurred extreme disdain and even hatred for missionaries. Subsequent to Mao's coming to power, all foreign missionaries were chased out of the country and China's giant doors were slammed shut in the face of missionary endeavor. Thirty years of closed-door policies and self-seclusion have made China poor and backward. The government tried to turn the tide by introducing policies advocating reform and openness, to nurture the economy, and to attract foreign investors. Despite these positive developments, foreign missionaries are officially still prohibited from entering China's missions harvest fields. They can only try to access our country with secular professions such as English teachers, businesspeople, teachers of science and technology, and other fields. The government may be able to formally reject foreign missionaries, but they cannot turn away those with proper secular status. Thus, today in China's major cities and governmental departments there are many tentmaking foreign missionaries. They have been channels of God's blessings to the Chinese church, but have simultaneously also created not a few problems for the local churches.

Not too long ago, I set out to survey the church situation in Eastern China. What I saw broke my heart and forced me into deep reflection. The churches in this region were established during the 1990's, when brothers and sisters in Christ were driven by the fire of God's Spirit and loved one another as they together served with great evangelistic fervor. Not only were churches established, evangelistic teams were assembled and one-year training schools set up as they nurtured a generation of leaders and constantly dispatched workers to preach the Gospel. Churches were quickly built up, and the saved were daily added to their ranks as the brethren focused on the plentiful harvest field of souls. However, trouble was brewing beneath the surface. Facing a lack of qualified instructors, suitable training materials and sufficient funds, their co-workers had little choice but to import teachers from overseas. For a while, this stemmed the tide and helped consolidate their ministries. However, not long after, these foreign missionaries started teaching their own brand of "truth." Hailing from different denominational traditions, they saw things from varying perspectives. Very unfortunately from the onset, these foreign teachers lobbied students in a bid to further their denominational interests. Worse still, some went so far as to manipulate ignorant and youthful trainees into mutual slander, rebuking and attacking one another such that the churches were split into many opposing factions. These apprentices became instigators of conflict and jealousy, so-called "heroes of turmoil." This approach from the church outside China is both incomprehensible and unacceptable to me and our leaders. Sadly, many co-workers resigned from their ministerial positions and withdrew from this cacophony for quiet reflection.

Much havoc was wrought among the churches; some came in the name of training but ended up drawing people away. Others used money and reputation to attract followers. Some have even openly "bought" churches in transactions, complete with contracts and signatures. The denominations have promised to support the local ministries financially and in return, not only do they want the Chinese churches under their control, but church names are changed and tithes submitted to the denomination so that they can claim a massive jump in its constituent churches and membership. China Gospel Fellowship would never dare sell out our churches in this manner, but others have done so, either unwittingly or because of the promised financial resources. This very unfortunate interface with the unregistered churches in China has led to many Chinese groups looking upon anyone from outside with great suspicion and there are some who will have nothing to do with the church outside, despite great sums of money being offered. What a sad commentary. How unfortunate that we, as the Body of Christ, have arrived at this point. On behalf of my brothers and sisters in China, I would ask the church outside to changes its ways and only enter China as servants and acknowledge their Chinese brothers and sisters as equals and not as the "lesser" brother or sister.

I often think to myself: What is this all about? Are these people working for themselves? Are they working for the Lord? Or are they working for their denominations? Should we receive them? Should we reject them? Often, we unconsciously get entangled in disputes and debates over the validity of having foreign missionaries on Chinese soil. Which is the better option? My heart wrestled with this paradox and I could not help but ask: What path must the church in China take? One with closed doors? One marked by openness? To close our doors would stifle and dry up the message we preach due to lack of fellowship and communication with others. To be open, we run the risk of church splits and confusion with regard to the truth. We do not wish to lose sight of God's unique way of leading the church in China.

According to the Bible, the church takes form universally, locally and in homes. The universal church has existed since her founding and encompasses all saints, whether in heaven or on earth, regardless of nationality, language or race. All who have been born again are one in Christ, under the jurisdiction of Christ, the head of the church, as we together constitute members of one body (Galatians 3:27-28; Ephesians 1:22-23). Biblical examples of local churches include those in Rome, Corinth and the seven in Asia Minor (1 Corinthians 1:2; Revelation 1:11). House churches include gatherings in the homes of Aquila and Priscilla, Philemon and Apphia (Romans 16:3-5; Philemon 1-2).

Now that the churches have already taken local form, they must strive to serve one another. The church in China needs help from brothers and sisters overseas. Yet, the lead roles must remain with the local leaders. They must be respected according to God's established hierarchy of church leadership. Foreign missionaries must go through the proper channels as they seek to make contact, assist, and cooperate with the Chinese churches. They must respect and support the Chinese church, understanding that the church in China is firmly rooted on Chinese soil as she blossoms for the Lord. She must neither be stifled nor tempted with financial incentives, such that she becomes subject to one's denominational body. The house churches in China have already been exempt from the bondage of denominationalism. Why now add this unnecessary burden upon her?

I am not in favor of people like Diotrephes who love to be first and refuse to show hospitality to true brethren (3 John 9). Church leadership must always be willing to receive visitors from afar. On the other hand, our stance on the truth must be firm as we carefully discern between right and wrong. Otherwise, we may unknowingly invite those into China who, like Diotrephes, want only to be first. We also must stand guard against heretical cults, not allowing them to infiltrate our ranks, thereby ruining both ourselves and our churches. The church must never turn away those who truly love and serve the Lord, or we will give up a great blessing. However, we must bear in mind that reckless reception will lead to turmoil and hinder the desire to do good deeds. The Bible has clearly listed seven criteria for unity (Ephesians 4:3-6), which may serve as a guideline. Further, using letters of recommendation is another possible avenue to protect us from those with mixed or wrong motives (Romans 16:1-2; 1 Corinthians 16:10-11; Philippians 2:25; Colossians 4:7, 9). We must always be prudent and discerning (Matthew 24:4; 1 Thessalonians 5:11) as we remember the biblical characteristics of false teachers (Jude 11-13; 2 Peter 2:1-3). Thus, we learn to discern and distinguish, holding firmly to the form of God's holy and righteous Word while recognizing the need to comprehend truth as all-encompassing and balanced, not the result of forced nor faulty interpretation. Neither must we universalize particular personal experiences into new rules and try to propagate and impose them on other believers.

God has established watchmen in every region to build up His churches through a team of co-workers. They are the respected elders in the house of God, loved and adored by brothers and sisters. In order to allow for a smooth development in our ministries, local churches will do well to inform and consult their church leaders before receiving overseas missionaries. You must interact with them and be certain of their beliefs, motives, and origins. Thereafter, you may confidently receive them. This is proper church procedure. We hope that the house churches in China will see tremendous progress without turmoil, but stable within her own ranks while maintaining cordial and cooperative contacts with others. In this spirit of camaraderie, we can together pioneer new horizons for the tremendous evangelistic harvest fields in China, so that we may work toward fulfilling God's Great Commission.

THE BATTLE FOR UNITY

CHAPTER VII

Church unity is God's will, the Bible's teaching, the hopeful prayer of generations of saints, and the desire of our Lord Jesus Christ before He left this world when He prayed:

> *Holy Father, protect them by the power of your name—the name you gave me—so that they may be one as we are one...My prayer is not for them alone. I pray also for those who will believe in me through their message, that all of them may be one, Father, just as you are in me and I am in you. May they also be in us so that the world may believe that you have sent me. I have given them the glory that you gave me, that they may be one as we are one: I in them and you in me. May they be brought to complete unity to let the world know that you sent me and have loved them even as you have loved me.*
>
> ***John 17:11, 20-23***

The truth concerning ecclesial unity is familiar to every preacher and continually preached, but also very difficult to actualize.

After 1949, all foreign missionaries were gradually expelled from China, which marked the end of an era of Christian denominationalism brought about by the various foreign missionary societies. From 1950 till 1980, China was dominated by the ebb and tide of consecutive political movements, but the most vicious of these was the Cultural Revolution. It drove the entire church toward underground meetings. During that time, we might say that the Chinese church was characterized by house meetings. In the early 1980s, the TSPM came into favor as the government implemented a series of leftist policies and imposed the "15 Prohibitions." These were contrary to biblical truth, and Christians found them extremely difficult to accept. In addition, the TSPM leadership advocated "new theology" and lacked true Christian beliefs. Consequently, the house churches and the Three-Self churches ceased all interaction with each other, a stalemate that continues to this day.

Other problems arose within the ranks of the house churches. Lack of communication and collective consensus on biblical truth led to the increasing independence of individual groups as each labored feverishly to spread the good news outward. As a result, many new sects appeared which were still mostly orthodox but some had turned extremist or even heretical. In the mid-1990s, some co-workers who loved the Lord took note of the crisis, and traveled all over China in a bid to gather the more influential house church leaders for fellowship and discussion on church unity. Everyone realized the importance of unity, for it fulfilled God's desire, stopped ecclesial infighting, propagated the Gospel, complemented each others' strengths and weaknesses, committed one another to sink or swim together, and prevented the influx of heresy. Everyone also agreed to maintain contact in the future. After the meeting, we enacted a few important measures:

1. Clarify individual church's creedal beliefs and organizational structure
2. Ensure that key leaders keep close contact and learn from each other
3. Mutually exchange theological literature to avoid self-innovation and self-exaltation
4. Mutually select a generally accepted set of hymns for communal learning and singing
5. Maintain current church management models
6. Mutually respect each other's affiliations without mutual interference
7. Mutually acknowledge each other's ministry boundaries and co-exist peacefully
8. Mutually accept and honor individual understandings of the truth
9. Maintain and continue to strive for ecclesial unity in Christ, and
10. Prudently minister when crossing into another church's ministry backyard

In recent years, we have had numerous such gatherings for interaction but have yet to see any major results because everyone has a different understanding of unity. They consider denominations to be historical artifacts that arose under special circumstances in the past. To try to do away with denominations altogether is hardly a viable option, but neither is exalting one's own brand of Christianity while belittling brothers and sisters who do not minister alongside oneself. It is both unloving and irresponsible to reject members of Christ's body who truly love the Lord. The churches in China all distinctly realize that many extremists and heretics have been shaped by a lack of fellowship and mutual correction. With regard to issues of mergers and organizational structures, all are agreed that a learning process is necessary. Organizational uniformity is not equivalent to ecclesial unity, which is an essential oneness in spiritual life. Three foundational slabs are crucial to accomplishing true unity:

1. Centered on Christ: Unity must have Christ at its core, not human effort—not an externalized organization, but an internalized essence of spiritual life. Unity achieved through human labor is unreliable because inherent in human hearts is an insatiable lust for power and control. The church must exist to magnify the Lord, with Christ as the object and nucleus of Christian ministry and fellowship. Such unity is pleasing to the Lord. As the apostle Paul said:

> *If you have any encouragement from being united with Christ, if any comfort from his love, if any fellowship with the Spirit, if any tenderness and compassion, then make my joy complete by being like-minded, having the same love, being one in spirit and purpose. Do nothing out of selfish ambition or vain conceit, but in humility consider others better than yourselves. Each of you should look not only to your own interests, but also to the interests of others.*
>
> ***Philippians 2:1-4***

2. Established upon Love: In his discourse on church unity, the apostle Paul wrote that the church "builds itself up in love" (Ephesians 4:16). Over the past few decades, the church in China has undergone a tumultuous baptism of extraction, destruction and oppression. Today, many who share this burden in the Lord ask the same questions: "How shall we establish the Chinese church? How can we achieve church unity?" There is only one answer: Be established in love. Yet, how difficult it is to live out this "love"!

Within the Three-Self Patriotic Movement, those hungry for power and fame resort to mutual backstabbing and clandestine attacks, even to the extent of mutual hatred and wish for mutual extinction. There is little contact between the house churches and the Three-Self Church because the differences and contradictions run too deep. For many decades, the TSPM has repeatedly framed and oppressed the house churches, bringing much pain and suffering. The house churches consider the TSPM to be in doctrinal turmoil, with relatively few true believers in their midst. Such views have seriously hurt those who truly believe in Jesus within the TSPM.

Many contradictions exist among the house churches themselves with regard to questions such as faith and beliefs, overlaps in pastoral zoning, and methods of ministry. Such differences in opinions have hindered table-talks and honest discussions. Today, many in the church talk about love but few actually live it out. At its essence, this is an issue of life. Those who lack spiritual life can never actualize God's sacred love. Those who possess eternal life in Christ simply love as an outflow of who they are.

With regard to the TSPM, we must distinguish between them and the church. The TSPM is a political movement and entity, not the church. The church of Jesus Christ, on the other hand, is not a political organization. We must reach out in love to those within TSPM ranks who have truly trusted in Jesus and not reject them. Obstacles need to be overcome if we are to attain unity. All who share in God's redemption are members of one body regardless of their denomination or church affiliation. These people share with us a common life. Spiritually, we are one church, the body of our Lord Jesus Christ. Thus, we must love one another.

3. United in Truth: True unity must be built upon a foundation of common beliefs. As the Bible says, we are to "reach unity in the faith" (Ephesians 4:13). This is truth recorded in the Bible as God's Word. Generations of Christians in all parts of the world have broadly accepted certain doctrinal creeds as benchmark summaries of biblical truth and the Christian faith. In November 1998, the leaders of a few representative house churches drafted a declaration of faith as a foundation for both church unity and mutual fellowship. To stand firm in the truth, the church must build itself upon the foundation of the apostles and prophets, exalt the Bible as the absolute measure of truth, consult theological works of the past, and avoid private or twisted interpretations of the Word. Scripture should normally interpret itself in conformity to context. Personal insights and experiences cannot ultimately replace God's truth. We must be approved and unashamed workmen of God who correctly handle the word of truth (2 Timothy 2:15).

In principle, the church must constantly seek to increase her tolerance and level of acceptance of brethren who differ from us in various aspects of the Christian faith. Pride, self-exaltation, stubbornness and prejudices ought to be taboo. We must earnestly pursue the seven guidelines of Christian unity:

> *Be completely humble and gentle; be patient, bearing with one another in love. Make every effort to keep the unity of the Spirit through the bond of peace.*
>
> ***Ephesians 4:2-3***

MAKING THE LEAP FROM VILLAGES TO THE CITY

Evangelism in the farming communities began with one-on-one engagements. Those who were born again and saved gladly shared the Gospel message with those around them. God also manifested Himself through the transformed lives of believers and, in many cases, with healings, exorcisms, and miraculous signs and wonders. The villages were unique in that governmental scrutiny was relatively loose and neighbors loved to interact with one another, and religious concepts were not uncommon. During less intensive phases of the agricultural season, Christian villagers would visit neighbors or relatives. Through such local habits, the Gospel spread, to the extent that entire families were coming to the Lord simultaneously and in countless cases, entire villages turned to Christ. Believing parents gladly dedicated their children to the Lord's ministry. After some simple form of instruction and training, they became vibrant members of the evangelistic army.

In the three months before and after the spring festival, villages located in the Central Plains face a harsh winter, when all agricultural activities cease. This is the lightest part of the farming season, but the busiest for Christian believers. Brothers and sisters gather together for the commencement of "Gospel Month" events. When it first started, preachers would talk about evangelistic strategies and give out some Gospel tracts. The brethren would then fast and pray and thereafter seek prospects for evangelism by proactively visiting non-believers. Through loving care and concern, and constant contact, they passed on God's great love and the truth of the Gospel to them. Within one month, the numbers at the house church exploded.

Thereafter, those who had been called by God came together to form a "Gospel mission team" with the aim of reaching all corners of China with the good news. Some brothers and sisters remained in the villages. Others entered the cities while still others ventured to live amidst the minority tribespeople. Evangelizing in the villages saw much success since the environment was familiar, and churches were quickly established. In the years that followed, we moved from small groups to families to local churches to pastoral zones, which culminated in team ministries and missionary dispatches in all directions. Our numbers kept growing as management and pastoral personnel were assigned to all levels of the organizational hierarchy. This church growth cycle repeated itself in various locations, and numerous mission teams were formed. The church used various means and ways to bring people to the Lord, through Gospel meetings, Bible studies, prayer meetings, healing services, worship services, children's ministries, fellowship gatherings, youth meetings, sister fellowships, and other outreaches. In this manner, needs at all levels could be met.

Believers became strongly rooted in their faith and as their spiritual lives grew, so the church expanded and stabilized.

Compared to ministry in the villages, evangelization in the cities is much more difficult. There are many differences between cities and villages:

1. time is of the essence
2. higher cultural standards
3. a sense of superiority
4. reluctance to interact with others
5. confined places of dwelling, and
6. stricter legislation on non-residents

All these factors contribute to hindering a breakthrough in our city ministries. Initially, some brothers and sisters could only minister in the suburbs. Once they had established their suburban ministries, they hoped to make use of their relatives residing in the cities as steppingstones to minister within the city limits. Some did business with their hometown acquaintances. Through eating, living and working together, Christian meetings were organized. Others would begin as independent entrepreneurs. With legitimate status, not only could meetings be held at their offices, they could also be self-sustaining. Still others would enroll in university campuses with the help of connections, and evangelize while they studied. As entrance requirements are lowered, more high school graduates become eligible for university studies. Based on the current state of affairs, the house church needs younger brethren to further their education in universities and thereby improve the quality of church co-workers. With better-trained talent, the church will become better rounded and more solidly grounded. Besides, such a move would open up opportunities for evangelism on campus.

We estimate that, Lord willing, if ten people were to enroll at a university each year for a four-year program and each were to lead five people to Christ during their course of studies, we would have at least 60 graduates after four years. If things go as planned, it is foreseeable that a sizeable group of Christian intellectuals could be formed. Since university students are relatively more innocent, open-minded and influenced by Western culture, they are prime candidates to accept the Gospel message.

Our greatest obstacle is the high tuition fees. Each student needs to pay around 10,000 renminbi ($1,200 USD) annually. In light of the current global economic downturn, it appears that our wonderful plan is in danger of premature death. Recently, I chatted with a university student and asked her about life on campus. She said, "In this past year of learning, I have grown in knowledge in all aspects. I am ranked within the top seven among my peers, and also participated in student gatherings of around 200, where I made many friends. Personally, I have led five people to Christ." After I listened to her testimony, I was very moved. Within a year, she had accomplished her "assignment" that was supposed to take four years. But when I remembered the financial pressures our church was under, I could only pray silently to God, "May the Lord have mercy and meet their needs. Please don't allow their scholarly pursuits and ministerial endeavors on campus to be disrupted."

As for our work among the minority tribes, since commencing in 1994, progress has been less than ideal. We have identified a few major factors:

1. most minority tribespeople reside in mountainous regions and are very poor and backward
2. they reside too far from the main passageways of travel, which becomes tedious in terms of cost and travel time
3. without suitable vocations, surviving in their midst is a tough task, and
4. disparities in cultural practices and language create barriers and difficulties in adaptation

Despite these obstacles, we have managed to establish a few churches among the minority tribes. We strongly believe that saving the nations is God's desire. If even Western missionaries could preach the Gospel to the minority tribespeople, it ought to be much easier for Chinese Christians. However, such ministry has a long learning curve, where personal experiences and strategies must be constantly evaluated and revised. Various avenues of consideration are both possible and necessary for our missionaries: agricultural management, medical and welfare services, living in their midst, nurturing local preachers, ministering based on biblical principles, respecting local customs, and establishing churches. May the good news become widespread among them! May revival come!

MIGRATORY MISSIONS

CHAPTER VIII

In 1999, the Chinese government rallied the nation to develop westward. The church too saw the ministerial needs in the western parts of the country, which were further from the Central Plains and had lower standards of living. Although we had preached the Gospel there and established a few churches, we found it difficult to stabilize our ministries due to distance, insufficient funds, lack of pastors, heretical disturbances and other challenges. All these factors contributed to stifling our developmental plans.

Migratory missions focuses on grafting missionaries into the local culture and preaching the Gospel through both word and deed, which differs from our previous conventional strategies of evangelizing as one travels. As we shared this new vision with our church members, we emphasized four major aspects:

1. Origination and Transmission of Vision: We started sharing about migratory missions in 1995. At that time, our church had started sending local Chinese church planters/missionaries to various parts of the country. Under the guidance of the Holy Spirit, we caught the vision of migratory missions as a missiological strategy. Hence, we looked into the Bible to see what it had to say concerning migratory missions. For example, Abraham was called out from Ur of the Chaldeans into the promised land of Canaan. This was the earliest recorded account of migration. Also, the entire Israelite nation came out of Egypt and entered Canaan. This was a large-scale migration to occupy unclaimed land. Further, our Lord Jesus Christ left His heavenly home, was incarnated and lived among us so that He may fulfill His Father's mission for Him. This was the greatest act of migratory missions in the entire history of human civilization.

Through examining and studying the biblical examples of migratory missions, we saw the potential impact this strategy could possibly have in China. Thus, in sharing our vision for missions with everyone, we placed our emphasis on migration as we defined it. For most of our co-workers, missions was then but a dream, because it seemed that the Chinese church was still a long way from fulfilling such a vision. In other words, circumstances for the house churches in China appeared not to be conducive for migratory missions.

Nonetheless, we continued to share our vision, whether during co-worker meetings or gatherings with various local churches. Whenever the topic of missions cropped up, we never failed to mention migratory missions. Be it in the pulpit or just visiting together, we discussed this strategy so that brothers and sisters could become better acquainted with its importance. All of a sudden, various local churches caught the wave and started propagating this vision. Many people were moved and dedicated themselves to become 21st-Century migratory missions warriors/church planters for the Lord. The church also began praying concerning strategic actualization.

Later on, one of our co-workers was arrested for sharing this vision. Under confinement, he was physically without freedom to actualize the vision, so he fervently prayed about it. When he received news in jail that his co-workers were still transmitting this vision, he was greatly comforted. During those two years behind bars, he had spent lots of time pondering and conceptualizing migratory missions. Once released, many people assumed that he would never again preach the same message. Contrary to expectations, his very first message after leaving prison was on migratory missions. He said, "Not only will I preach about it, I will now begin to actualize this vision." In 1998, propagation of this vision came to a crescendo. Practically every co-worker and believer under our pastoral care was deeply convicted of its critical importance, and prayed fervently for its fulfillment. Migratory missions had truly become common knowledge.

2. Function and Purpose of Migratory Missions: Migratory missions holds many advantages with regard to the transmission of the Gospel in closely-related or radically-different cultures. Chinese missionaries will live among minority tribal peoples and seek to influence them with their Christian lives through God's love. Furthermore, these missionaries will have sufficient time devoted to patiently explaining the Gospel message so that the locals may better comprehend and accept the good news of God's love as manifested in salvation through the cross. Prior to the communist liberation, many foreign missionaries traversed oceans to immerse themselves in the poor, backward and ultra-conservative cultures of China. They took the Gospel inland and lived alongside the almost primitive members of minority tribes, thereby testifying of the love of our Lord Jesus Christ. Their efforts have not been in vain. The lives and ministries of these migratory missions warriors have borne much fruit on Chinese soil. Countless people accepted the good news. Entire tribes, such as the Miao people group, have been known to succumb to the love of Christ, which supports our thesis that migratory missions is an effective strategy for accomplishing missions to closely-related and radically different cultures. Today, migratory missions couples are sowing the seeds of the kingdom in areas of greatest need. Before long, they too will see the fruit of their labor.

Through our migratory missions, missionary teams undergo a gradual process of maturation and stabilization. To begin with, most missionaries selected are couples who have been married for many years. Not only are they better rounded in their spiritual maturity, these couples are experienced in ministry and are constitutionally strong in coping with the stresses of life. Moreover, husband and wife can complement one another's strengths as they work together for the furtherance of the Gospel ministry.

Why did we not pick young, unmarried people? Quite simply, most young people are preoccupied with matters of choosing a life mate or preparing for marriage, which can allow them to be distracted and add a significant amount of stress. To a greater or lesser extent, one's life of ministry is inevitably affected. Often, the realities of such dilemmas turn many back from full-time ministry. There have been some who were forced by marital and family responsibilities to seek a different vocation and unfortunately, some have even left their ministries and turned toward the world.

Over the years, in the course of ministry, brothers and sisters in the church could hardly provide for the needs of house church co-workers. Despite evident biblical teaching in this respect, the churches had insufficient resources to actualize it. This continues to be the most limiting challenge we face. In spite of this, our campaign for migratory missions spurred everyone to sacrifice and contribute their widow's mites' worth in support of co-worker needs as they carried out the church's ministry. In the process, everyone also understood truths on tithing and that those who preach the Gospel depend on the Gospel for their sustenance. Evangelists can continue their ministries because of such "widow's mites." While carrying out their mission, these evangelists could also emulate the apostle Paul in "tentmaking." Not only could they then sustain their own needs, they would also lighten the burdens of other co-workers and the church as a whole.

3. Execution and Effects of Migratory Missions: In view of these functions and purposes, coupled with the prayers of brothers and sisters, our co-workers felt that the time was right to launch this domestic missions program in September 1999.

Migratory missionaries have to undergo a rigorous selection process as well as training, so as to ensure that the workers sent out would be of use to the Lord. These couples had to have the following qualifications:

- clear sense of God's calling
- counting the costs involved
- dedication to the cause of migratory missions
- complete training and equipping in the truth, having enrolled in both short-term study and correspondence courses
- total immersion in this ministry and
- ability for self-survival

Without these attributes, they may well regret their decision the moment adverse circumstances come upon them. That would leave their endeavors half-complete, and the Gospel ministry would thereby be stalled.

At that time, we asked God for three signs: (1) we asked God to prepare for us 30 such couples; (2) we asked God to prepare for us 30 more couples who would commit financially to support migratory missions; and (3) we asked God to prepare for us suitable training materials and suitable locations to conduct the necessary training. The Lord confirmed our convictions by providing us with training materials and venues, 30 missionary couples and enough resources to cover six months of ministry. Our budget for the remaining six months of that year had also been met through God's provision. In early November 1999, we gathered these committed missionary couples for training, and then sent them out to various mission fields.

Many of them became pioneers in places where the Gospel had yet to be preached, such as the remote regions, the minority tribes and also the cities. More precisely, these locations included Tibet, Qinghai, Xinjiang, Yunnan, Guizhou, Guangxi, Sichuan, Guangdong, Hainan, Fujian, Jiangxi and Hunan. When we sent them out, we designated a broad area for each couple, hence trusting the Spirit of God to lead them in the specifics of their ministry location. The first group of missionaries focused mainly on prospects of similar and distinct cultures within our national boundaries.

Since this was our first attempt at migratory missions, we had our reservations; so much was probationary, with the missionaries returning home biannually. Upon returning, they fellowshipped and shared concerning their individual situations. This greatly helped the church in better supporting their ministries, especially through prayer. From May 20-23, 2003, after a long and arduous journey, our migratory missions warriors came home from their fields and gathered somewhere in the Central Plains to fellowship and share their experiences. This gathering was of tremendous help to the co-workers involved in migratory missions. From then onward, we planned for them to return annually for such sharing sessions

The leadership determined that depending on the unique situations in their respective mission fields, these missionaries might be either full-time evangelists or part-time tentmakers. Each person must maximize his or her gifts and specialties so as to better accomplish the missions tasks.

For the initial six months, our missionaries were either working with existing churches or pioneering new ministries. We believe that forming alliances is a stepping-stone especially important when entering uncharted waters in ministry. Although great visible results are not yet evident, we trust that their work has God's blessings. Some of them have already made contact with local churches, which serves as a base for subsequent ventures into the minority tribes or unevangelized regions. Others have already pioneered new ministries and established churches. In more concrete terms, their ministries have withstood pressure on many fronts. For instance, they have faced attacks from certain Three-Self churches, persecution from local governmental authorities, linguistic obstacles, assaults from demonic sources, and interference by heretical groups. Amidst such adverse circumstances, things have hardly been easy going for our missionaries. Still, we strongly believe that, buffered by the prayers of the saints in the various churches, they will be more than conquerors through the Author and Perfector of our faith, Jesus Christ.

Furthermore, since these six months had basically been occupied by liaison and pioneering work, communication with us as the sending church was difficult. Hence, we could only send co-workers to visit very few locations. In the future, our ministry in migratory missions needs to see closer teamwork between the senders and the sent, so that their work may be strengthened. We plan to organize itinerant teaching teams that will constantly travel across the country to help meet our missionaries' various practical needs through theological literature and multi-media resources. This supporting ministry needs more co-workers and prayers. In essence, praying and contributing financially to this ministry is already a form of involvement. We hope that the brothers and sisters in the various local churches will become actively involved in the Lord's work. Upon hearing news about this ministry, many members of the body of Christ both here and abroad were deeply moved. Through their financial gifts, they supported this wonderful ministry of missions.

In principle, financially our church has pledged to support the church planters/migratory missionaries for three years, after which they are expected to be financially independent, surviving by faith in God's direct providence. Although we as leadership made this commitment, it was entirely a faith commitment, as we had no foreseen way to provide for them out of our meager resources. Deep in our hearts, we knew God would provide and would multiply whatever we could gather. We felt that somehow, He would do so by placing the responsibility and burden on the shoulders of brothers and sisters in Christ outside of China. Looking back, we see that is exactly how our Heavenly Father provided.

In the year 2000, when our affiliated churches heard that we had dispatched 30 couples for migratory missions, they too responded to God's call and started propagating this vision by training and sending out workers. Thus, a vibrant wave of missionary migration began. On the eve of the wheat harvest that year, a particular church in the Central Plains dispatched 20 couples for migratory missions.

Migratory missions must seem anything but extraordinary outside of China, but to us Chinese Christians who live amidst very different circumstances, it is an important step. The very fact that Chinese house churches today can embark on this historic journey into missions is itself an amazing miracle performed by our God. If God were not with us, we would not have been able to do such a thing because this was a pathway without any guarantees of success. We could approach it only with faith and love in response to God's calling.

4. Perfections and Projections of Migratory Missions: With the onset of missions ministries, some of our warriors in migratory missions would be required to learn the languages of minority tribes on their own. However, we planned that when they first approached the minority peoples, they would use Mandarin Chinese (since practically all the young people know it). Thereafter, they would communicate the Gospel message through translators. Thus, despite situations where language is a barrier, it is still possible for evangelistic ministries to proceed. Nonetheless, deeper impact would require learning the tribal languages and understanding their social norms. If our missionaries have a burden for a particular tribe, then they must learn the language of that tribe on their own after they have started ministering among the locals. By living and interacting with the tribespeople, their learning through immersion would be much easier. For now, our church is unable to focus on training our co-workers in each specific minority language, but there is an urgent need to decipher, among other things, their cultural practices and religious beliefs. Prior to sending out our first group of missionaries, we dispatched co-workers to scout certain minority regions in a bid to better understand how each tribe was geographically distributed, thereby providing helpful information to our missionaries as they seek to evangelize their respective target groups.

In trying to empathize with the concerns of migratory missionary couples, our church is now paying heed to questions regarding their children's education as well as financial support. These issues are difficult to handle due to the economic and political situation in China, as well as other factors. As a result, this continues to be very challenging and in many cases impossible for us to address. These are concerns that require active participation from the churches at large. Only then can these missionaries be adequately provided for and free of anxiety as they wholeheartedly fight the good fight in the name of our Lord.

After we had dispatched our first missionaries, more couples responded to God's call for migratory missions. Many inquired as to when the second group would be dispatched. Tentatively, we plan to send out another 30 to 40 couples. This second group will possibly go to the fringe regions of Northwest and Northeast China, where the Gospel has barely penetrated. Still, our focus is on the minority people groups. Further, we will continue to propagate and consolidate this vision of migratory missions and we estimate that soon, many churches could possibly be sending out migratory missionaries.

While our immediate focus is on the minority tribes, we have also made preliminary plans for foreign missionary endeavors, especially to our bordering nations (e.g., Myanmar [Burma], India, North Korea and the Arabic countries). Although we have not actually started our foreign missions involvement, we are planning for some of our members to learn the Arabic language as a foundation for future ministry to the Arabs. We confidently proclaim that: "The church in China is preparing to carry the burden of the Gospel Mandate to the world in the 21st-Century."

(I understand there is much interest in the West in what is called the Back to Jerusalem Movement. Speaking as a leader of one of China's house church movements, I have observed that at this preliminary stage, the Back to Jerusalem Movement is more of a slogan than a movement.

We, of course, are committed to seeing the Gospel proclaimed throughout all the earth. Our primary work and commitment is to first reach China for Christ and as we prepare and the Lord allows, we will reach out to the minorities in China and then to bordering nations, but our focus remains to work the harvest fields in China while the fields are white.)

GREAT POVERTY PROVIDES GREAT OPPORTUNITY TO SHARE

From the fall of 2002 to the present, our church has begun to emphasize good works. This is something that Christians must essentially pursue with fervency. However, since the church is often under persecution, Christians tend to lose heart in this regard. I thought about the church during the time of the biblical apostles. They too were being persecuted; they too underwent severe and cruel treatment. Hence, the apostle Paul encouraged the churches in Galatia, saying:

> *Let us not become weary in doing good, for at the proper time we will reap a harvest if we do not give up. Therefore, as we have opportunity, let us do good to all people, especially to those who belong to the family of believers.*
>
> ***Galatians 6:9-10***

The apostle Peter also once wrote to the suffering church:

> *For it is God's will that by doing good you should silence the ignorant talk of foolish men.*
>
> ***1 Peter 2:15***

In many churches, specific people have been designated to take charge of good works, such as repairing public roads, caring for the poor, sheltering homeless children. Whatever has been neglected, Christians must show concern. Whatever nobody wants to do, Christians must step up and do. This greatly changed the world's perception of the church. Whereas they may have previously assumed that Christians were preoccupied with just singing and praying, they could now witness with their own eyes how the church blesses society through practical acts of kindness. Some local Party officials have even awarded banners of commendation to churches so that they may hang these banners in their places of worship.

Many village churches have also organized training seminars teaching the villagers on better techniques of raising chickens, sheep, and pigs and planting edible fungi. Other lessons teach machine repair, welding, cooking, and other skills. These practical skills have helped many poor families solve their problems with daily sustenance. The Lord's name is glorified and praised in the world. The church adopts a refreshing stance before the world, through which the good news has found new avenues into hundreds and thousands of families.

PARASITIC DEPENDENCE VERSUS SELF-SUSTENANCE OF CHURCH WORKERS

China is a major agricultural nation. Thus, it is little surprise that the house churches of China have their roots in the farming communities. When we first started evangelizing, most people walked, while those who were better off would ride on bicycles, weaving through nearby counties and cities within a radius of two to three hundred miles. As the good news spread and more people came to Christ, more and more local churches were established. Out of their love for the evangelists, brothers and sisters in the Lord started making financial gifts to help support them.

Before 1990, church offerings did not amount to much. Due to the political situation, no one really taught on giving. If we even got close to a message on giving, it most likely occurred in the context of someone making a meager thanksgiving offering out of gratitude for a miraculous healing of some sort in answer to his or her prayers. Moreover, living standards were very poor in the villages. When even daily sustenance was a problem to be solved, the topic of giving hardly seemed relevant. After 1990, our ministries in neighboring provinces began to make progress. Since traveling expenses were naturally higher for longer journeys, stipends for evangelists also increased. This, however, put the church in a difficult position. Most of our evangelists were single and therefore without family commitments. Even those with families could not do much to support their spouse or children apart from helping out a little with farming duties. The church was never in the habit of financially supporting our evangelists due to reasons such as:

1. the poverty level of churches in farming communities
2. amidst a political environment marked by constant persecution, the tendency to avoid slanderous labels of "profiting under the guise of religion"
3. the nature of the church as a "citizens' army" and "laity movement" whereby all ministerial positions were considered equal and professional pastors were unheard of, and
4. the lack of teaching that *"those who preach the gospel should receive their living from the gospel"* *(1 Corinthians 9:14)*

A crisis arose with regard to church ministry and the propagation of the Gospel. How will single evangelists cope once they get married? Middle-aged full-time workers in local churches face the following problems: children's education, medical bills of relatives, and maintenance and repair expenses for broken-down houses. These families have contributed so much already for the Lord's sake, including financially, hosting visiting evangelists, laboring on itinerant ministries, and even going to jail and getting fined. Many times, they come to their wits' end when contemplating how to carry on such a lifestyle. Not a few were thus forced to leave their ministries and move elsewhere in order to make a living.

There was the case of one family who loved the Lord, received others and opened up their home for church meetings. When brothers and sisters gathered, the husband would preach while the wife would serve the guests. As the house was on the verge of collapse, they had to borrow money to make the necessary repairs. Due to their unpaid debts, creditors often came knocking. Failure to pay their dues would shame the Lord's name, but paying on time would mean giving up their ministries and moving elsewhere to find jobs. This couple was caught in the unenviable dilemma of leaving or staying, which eventually led to many domestic squabbles between them. Such cases are definitely not isolated examples among the house churches in China. It would be a tremendous shame for such unfortunate tragedies to continue where God's workers are lost to worldly pursuits. Younger generations of seminarians may be discouraged and decide to turn their backs on full-time ministry. Older generations may also hesitate when encouraging their children to dedicate their lives to serving the Lord.

This is an hour of critical need. When certain foreign missionaries enter China to carry out Gospel ministries, they witness with their own eyes the poverty level of the Chinese house churches, and they respond in three ways. Some are greatly moved by the great sacrifice and needs of the Church and they willingly make financial gifts to them. Some help with the daily expenses of evangelists; some express concern for missionary needs, while others focus on theological education. In this manner, such foreign aid has given both invaluable support and a great impetus toward the Chinese churches.

However, we also continue to be puzzled by how few actually help. Most come in, see the great suffering and poverty, meet with us, hear the stories and leave with great promises. They tell us they will return with help and then never return or return and neglect to help. Others come in to teach and we facilitate the meetings, call in our brothers and sisters from great distances, house and feed the foreign guests and then we learn we are to cover the very costly bills for travel, housing and feeding. It is not that we don't want to be able to do this. We simply don't have the funds for this. The foreign teacher goes home believing that he has given the Church in China what is so needed, "his teaching," and failed to understand what he has left behind.

Foreign financial assistance, provided appropriately is, on one hand, a huge blessing to the churches, allowing for the propagation of the Gospel, establishment of ministry teams, migratory missions, and theological training. On the other hand, the great danger is that it could result in parasitic dependence of Chinese co-workers on foreign aid.

After the year 2000, we faced crises on all sides. Funds were insufficient and many ministries already underway were unable to continue, which left the Lord's work half-finished. Numerous visions and plans were conceived but died of stillbirth. Training programs, already underway, had to be pruned back or cease altogether. Due to cultural disparities, there even arose sentiments of mutual suspicion. At the present time, we see a decline in assistance from foreign Christians. Possible reasons for this include:

1. the impression that the Chinese economy has already taken great strides forward
2. supporters themselves encounter financial difficulties
3. monetary aid has resulted in negative impact in certain situations
4. givers harbor ulterior motives of furthering their own careers in China, and
5. God Himself wishes for the churches in China to mature amidst these trials

All in all, Chinese churches must seriously consider moving toward the goal of self-sustenance. It is biblical teaching that churches be self-sustaining as a sign that they are spiritually healthy. Thus, church leaders would not lose sight of the fact that all members in Christ's body are mutually dependent. They can thereby better lead their members to make offerings for the sake of unity and a common vision for the Lord's ministry. Ministers would then be free of possible restrictions arising from financial dependence on outsiders; the church could avoid turmoil due to financial disputes; the government would lose their foothold to accuse the churches on monetary grounds; and church leaders would not lose their self-esteem because of money. We trust that God will open the door to this major breakthrough.

In the church, both full-time and tentmaking ministers must discern the distinct call of God upon their life and thus be steadfast in their respective vocations. Tentmakers are to do their utmost to make money through their own hard work so that they may have the means to help the needy. Full-time ministers are to focus on preaching and praying while depending on the church, or directly on individual believers, for provision. The Bible exhorts the believer:

Work, doing something useful with his own hands, that he may have something to share with those in need.

Ephesians 4:28

Anyone who receives instruction in the word must share all good things with his instructor.

Galatians 6:6

Do not muzzle an ox while it is treading out the grain.

1 Corinthians 9:9

The elders who direct the affairs of the church well are worthy of double honor, especially those whose work is preaching and teaching.

1 Timothy 5:17

Sometimes, while switching to a different ministry location or under special circumstances, full-time ministers can "make tents" to support themselves and their co-workers (Acts 18:1-4).

Our people must learn to devote themselves to doing what is good, in order that they may provide for daily necessities and not live unproductive lives.

Titus 3:14

However, such tentmaking work ought to be temporary. As circumstances change, the goal remains to revert to full-time ministry.

Preachers must teach the brethren how to handle their finances as faithful stewards, so that they may be rich in terms of doing good while supplying the needs of full-time ministers and actively involving themselves in church ministries. Tithing must be emphasized as an acknowledgement of God's sovereignty. In some sense, the tithe is "tax" paid to God, the portion assigned to His full-time workers. It is also an act of faith. God's workers must be content with sufficient food and clothing without complaint. Ministers must have these important attributes: contentment, thanksgiving, propriety in financial management, faithful reliance upon God and not men. Furthermore, they must be prudent, resolving to lead a simple life, preserving themselves from greed and refraining from competing with others and asking for higher salaries.

Ministers must also grow in their spiritual lives, gifts, knowledge and ministries as they seek to meet the spiritual needs of brothers and sisters in Christ. They must avoid becoming "rainless clouds," "waterless wells," "unfruitful trees" and "wicked servants" who are "lazy." Other hallmarks of God's servants include integrity, industry, honesty, faithfulness toward God's mission and preaching the complete biblical truth. Our hope is that the day will soon come when the church will have "washed off shame from her face, and smashed her bowl of beggary" by attaining the independence of self-sustenance. Even beyond that, we hope that the Chinese church will become a "giving" church, a channel of blessing to other churches in China and around the world.

HERESY AND TRUTH

CHAPTER IX

The gospel ministry grew tremendously in the various regions, but this created pastoral difficulties because brothers and sisters in church were relatively uncultured and had never undergone formal theological training. Furthermore, everyone ministered as tentmakers with little time for personal devotions, sermon preparation or visitations. This resulted in a situation whereby they "could give birth" and lead people to faith in the Lord, but they were weak in nurturing and discipleship. Around the country, many extremists and heretics also surfaced, such as the Shouters, Weeping Regeneration, Three Ranks of Servants, Two Taels of Wheat and others. Above all, the Eastern Lightning cult was the Chinese version of Satanism, posing a considerable threat to the churches. Some of our co-workers shared this common insight that in order to maintain revival in the church, we must strengthen training in the truth. In 1998, based on the state of the church and where we assessed our brethren needed strengthening, we edited three elementary textbooks: *Lessons on the Christian Faith, Lessons on Christian Living,* and *Lessons on Christian Ministry*. Subsequently, we also authored *"Questions and Answers on Christian Ethics and Morals."* Using these materials, we conducted training sessions. Thus, we strengthened the churches in their knowledge of basic Christian beliefs, modeled for them a Christian lifestyle, and guided them in ministerial strategy.

For this reason, we organized 20 to 30 training classes so that our younger brothers and sisters could be equipped. During one of our training sessions, I told them, "Based on our political climate, financial abilities, teacher credentials and pedagogical resources, it is not easy for us to conduct this kind of training. Still, we have to do it. Otherwise, it will be very difficult to preserve the church in the truth. Not only will we not overcome in spiritual warfare, but more and more people will be lost to heresy. In order to fill some of gaps, we need the young people in our churches to dedicate themselves to the ministry. By undergoing training, you can then become elite soldiers in Christ's army and fight the good fight under His banner."

STANDING ON FOUNDATIONAL BIBLICAL TRUTH AGAINST HERESY AND CULTS

As Jesus sat on the Mount of Olives, His disciples asked Him concerning signs indicating the end times. Jesus replied:

> *Watch out that no one deceives you. For many will come in my name, claiming, "I am Christ," and will deceive many.*
>
> **Matthew 24:4-5**

The apostle Peter also prophesied:

> *But there were also false prophets among the people, just as there will be false teachers among you. They will secretly introduce destructive heresies, even denying the sovereign Lord who bought them—bringing swift destruction on themselves. Many will follow their shameful ways and will bring the way of truth into disrepute.*
>
> **2 Peter 2:1-2**

China's unique circumstances have spawned numerous cults and heresies, bringing about theological confusion and threatening the well-being of the house churches. Since most members of the house churches came to faith through signs and wonders or through life testimonies, few among them had received systematic forms of theological training. Furthermore, the incredibly high congregation-to-pastor ratio created the ideal breeding ground for cultic movements as innocent believers warmly received any available preachers from abroad with little or no regard for their orthodoxy. Many fell into deception and sinful behavior. Others were "once bitten, twice shy" as they scrupulously excluded anyone with even minor discrepancies from their churches and branded true brothers and sisters in Christ as heretics. Of course, the government could not distinguish between orthodox and heretical Christian groups, so all non-Three-Self Patriotic Movement meetings were deemed heretical and viciously persecuted as cult groups.

Because of this, it is important for us to carefully distinguish between what is orthodox, extreme, heretical and cultic, so that we may avoid polarization or lose the essence of Christianity. For starters, every Christian must clearly understand what constitutes orthodox belief. In early church history, the Apostles' Creed, the Nicene Creed and the Athanasian Creed were widely circulated as accepted parameters of true Christian faith, not only outlining orthodoxy, but also delineating heresy. Key aspects of orthodox faith, such as the triune nature of God, the dual nature of Christ as both God and man, and salvation, were covered in these creeds. Later generations of Christians would draw from these statements of faith and delineate five rules of faith for determining heresy.

1. Do they believe that the true God is three Persons in one Godhead? (cf. Deuteronomy 6:4; Matthew 28:19; 2 Corinthians 13:14)
2. Do they believe that Jesus Christ was God fully incarnate in human flesh? (cf. 1 John 14; 1 John 4:3; 1 Timothy 2:5)
3. Do they believe that one is saved absolutely by justification through faith? (cf. Ephesians 2:8-9; Romans 3:23-28)
4. Do they believe that the Bible is the complete, absolute and highest authority governing both faith and practice? (cf. 2 Timothy 3:16; 2 Peter 3:15)
5. Do they manifest fruit (deeds) corresponding to their faith? (cf. Matthew 3:8; 7:15-18)

Boundaries drawn to distinguish extremists, unlike those excluding heretics, occur within the confines of the Christian faith. In other words, it is an internal matter, since both sides share the basic content of orthodox faith. They only differ because certain aspects are overly emphasized, leading to sectarianism, e.g., the Anabaptists (only baptism by immersion is correct, so those previously baptized in other ways must be re-baptized by immersion in order to join the group); in China, the "Suffering Perseverers Sect" (emphasized suffering and opposition to use of modern technology); the "Little Flock Hat-Wearing Sect"; and the "Weeping Born-Again Sect" among many others. We must seek to point out the errors in these extremist groups so that they may be corrected and reoriented through loving persuasion. Much faith and patience is required, coupled with firm warnings reminding them of the potential dangers of their extreme beliefs and practices. Through prayer, we ask for the Lord's mercy that, by the power of the Holy Spirit, these straying brethren will find their focus again.

The heretics are the true enemies of the church, the weeds among the wheat. They are false brethren cloaked in Christian garments whose actual beliefs are markedly different from those of orthodox Christianity. Their errors are foundationally wrong due to innovation, hence confusing and confounding the truth. If they deny the Trinity and turn the Triune God into a modalistic god in three stages of manifestation (i.e., the Father becomes the Son, and the Son becomes the Spirit), then they are heretical. Likewise, some affirm only the divinity and not the humanity of Jesus Christ or vice versa. Others rely on observance of the Law for their salvation. Still others even deny the Bible or lower its authority; for example, the Mormons, Jehovah's Witnesses, Shouters, Two Taels of Flour Sect and others. In the face of such heresies, the church must adopt strong measures in a bid to oppose and counter their attacks:

1. The church must appoint watchmen who will watchfully intercede on behalf of the church while paying close attention to the heretics' strategies and sounding the alarm whenever danger is imminent.
2. Christians must constantly consult the Bible and adhere to hermeneutical principles so that they may correctly divide the Word.
3. Christians must stand firm in their beliefs and not be swayed by winds of heresy.
4. The church must be organizationally healthy,

with good communication channels and all members watching for each other in working together as a team.

5. Whenever Christians encounter heretical harassment, common courtesy must take a back seat as they exalt the truth and earnestly contend for the faith.
6. Christians must constantly guard their hearts in absolute dependence on the Lord to overcome all trials and temptations.
7. Whenever Christians encounter unfamiliar preachers of little known background, prudence must be exercised before receiving them, lest Christians be deceived.

Cults are extremist heretical groups that may perhaps appear brandishing a Christian-like banner as a front for their disgraceful endeavors. They have a tight organizational structure with tight controls and strict beliefs, often resorting to unscrupulous means to achieve their ends: deception, lying, rumor-mongering, conning, mind-control, trickery, leader worship, greed, immorality, and violence. In recent years, cult groups have surfaced in many countries; for example, the Children of God in the United States, the Aum Shinrikyo cult in Japan, the Unification Church in South Korea, and the Eastern Lightning in China. These groups have wrought severe havoc in the lives of the common people. Yet, the Chinese government has no idea how to distinguish between the orthodox, extremist, heretical and cultic varieties of religious groups. Numerous house churches have been denied protection under Chinese law and have instead been branded as cultic. Such broad and baseless categorization has opened windows of opportunity for cultic activities to blossom. Many brethren have been kidnapped and hurt while others have fallen straight into their traps.

Hence, the church must adopt effective measures to preserve the purity of her faith while exposing the schemes of the Eastern Lightning cult, so that their plans to harm others may be thwarted:

1. Continually propagate messages warning everyone of the Eastern Lightning's threat to the welfare of the church.

2. Expose the undercover agents sent into the church by the Eastern Lightning. During meetings, we will declare in Jesus' name curses upon the self-proclaimed female Christ, cursing her cultic organization to dissolution and destruction, and cursing those who labor and speak on her behalf. Further, we must watch out for those "especially fervent seekers" who initially join the church.
3. Capture Eastern Lightning propagandists as a warning to others. If the authorities are willing, we will gladly cooperate with them.
4. Be especially prudent when dealing with foreign preachers. They must be formally introduced and have their ID number and home address taken down.
5. In the event that we are kidnapped by the cultists, we must immediately call for help. We would rather fall into the hands of the police than be captured by the Eastern Lightning.
6. Should we be kidnapped, we must watchfully pray and guard our hearts while maintaining adamant refusal to *listen, watch, think, debate or believe* anything they offer. This is the strategy of the "Five Won't." Beware lest you not fall into temptation.
7. Those recently released by their kidnappers must be temporarily suspended from ministry while undergoing personal interviews and honest interactions. Everyone should also love and care for them, thus helping them to cope emotionally and comprehend intellectually.
8. For those who have clearly understood that they have fallen victim to cultic attack, they must publicly testify and denounce the evil deeds of the Eastern Lightning, so as to reassure the church of their fidelity and regain the church's trust.
9. For those who remain hesitant, we must watchfully, lovingly and faithfully persuade them in a bid to rescue them from cultic dangers.
10. For those who have already been deceived and who refuse to repent, we must strike their names off our church rosters in the name of our Lord Jesus Christ, and hand them over to Satan.

CHINA'S FAMILIES IN TROUBLE

Human civilization began with the family; since ancient times, societies have been built around the family unit. The Chinese people are no exception, placing particular emphasis on familial values and morals. With the onset of reform, Chinese society has become increasingly open. The influx of many wonderful things from both the United States and Europe has also introduced a whole series of undesirables: sexual emancipation, homosexuality, premarital cohabitation, test marriages, and divorce. All this flooded Chinese society. The five core relationships which have traditionally defined Chinese families are now tattered and torn in the face of a major crisis. Divorce rates are increasing by the day, and premarital sex has become very common.

Our young people today hold frivolous attitudes toward sex, and even proclaim with joy, "This is a season of sexual emancipation, a season of free love, a time for revival of human nature, an occasion for eating, drinking, making merry and spending." Where romantic love is concerned, the motto is: "It doesn't matter how long it lasts, only that you've once possessed." This is their creed. They make friends without prudence in emulation of Western standards of getting acquainted, neither asking about age, marital status, residential address, vocation or religious belief. Whenever parents question their children on these matters, the younger generation will knit their brows and even exclaim. "It's none of your business!" Rebelliousness toward parents is a growing trend. The new generation is driven by independence, fashion, indifference, excitement and fun. Their lives revolve around discotheques, movie theaters, Internet cafes and liquor bars. Their self-centeredness is well summarized by a popular jingle: "Grandpa's heart is full of Mao Zedong, Daddy's heart is full of Grandpa, and their hearts are full of themselves." With the population explosion in China, the authorities have implemented a policy of Planned Parenthood. It is estimated that 40 percent of youth today come from single-child families. They are like the sun around which their planetary collections of relatives revolve, which has been called a "6-to-1" syndrome (i.e., one child to one set of parents and two sets of grandparents). Thus, many children grow up into selfish and proud brats.

The Bible teaches us:

> *Fathers, do not exasperate your children; instead, bring them up in the training and instruction of the Lord.*
>
> **Ephesians 6:4**

> *Children, obey your parents in the Lord, for this is right. "Honor your father and your mother"—which is the first commandment with a promise—"that it may go well with you and that you may enjoy long life on the earth."*
>
> **Ephesians 6:1-3**

Here, Paul instructs us on the responsibility of parents and the requirements of children. Parents must not stir up their children to anger, but ought to respect them as individuals without ridiculing, belittling or embarrassing them with harsh words. Without curbing their childhood innocence, parents can mold their character in the growing stages of life by teaching their kids to distinguish between right and wrong. This will instill in their young hearts the basic principles of life.

> *Train up a child in the way he should go, and when he is old he will not turn from it.*
>
> **Proverbs 22:6**

Parents are the first teachers of any child. Bring them up to fear the Lord and trust in Jesus, learning how to pray, respecting elders, loving the brethren, polite towards others, pure at heart and faithful in all endeavors. Refrain from harshly rebuking them, but seek to praise and encourage them to develop their potential. It is a delicate balance between reward and rebuke, between grace and justice. While children and parents ought to be friends most of the time, when kids have done wrong and need correction, parents have to maintain their stature of awe.

Children ought to demonstrate filial piety toward their parents. This is a commandment of God and a requirement stipulated in the Bible. It is also a human virtue, duty and responsibility. Christians must respect and obey their parents out of gratitude to them for their upbringing. Their strengths ought to be emulated, but Christ's love is often necessary to enable us to love them. Familial ethics according to the Bible lists God as first priority, because our Lord Jesus Christ instructed us:

> *If anyone comes to me and does not hate his father and mother, his wife and children, his brothers and sisters–yes, even his own life–he cannot be my disciple.*
>
> **Luke 14:26**

The Bible requires us as Christians in Ephesians 6:1 to: *Obey your parents in the Lord.*

We must comply with all parental demands that are not contrary to God's will. If they want us to worship idols or perform evil deeds, then we would rather offend them than offend God. Still, we must let them know our love toward them by persuading them with a reverential attitude of our Christian stance.

Family relations and ethics are of the utmost importance. Christian witness is lost if marital relationships are not cordial, if couples perpetually fight and quarrel, if daughters-in-law and mothers-in-law grow distant from one another, and if children run away from their homes. The next generation may reap the negative repercussions of these relational breakdowns, so much so that the serenity of a peaceful home becomes a living hell.

The Bible demands that husbands and wives love, honor and understand one another. Husbands must love their wives, and wives must respect their husbands. Couples should deal with each other in mutual honesty, trust, respect, courtesy, patience and love. Yet, love is more than mere feeling. Rather, love is a conscious choice, a lifelong promise to be kept, and a dedication of one's free will. The dating stage of boy-girl relationships is often filled with romantic fantasies which paint many ideal pictures of the future. However, once they enter the marital phase, practical problems begin to surface. Couples must then have the courage to shoulder the responsibilities and learn to complement one another while paying attention to emotional interchange and mutual understanding. Unrealistic dreams must be abandoned as mutual expectations are revised. Mutual self-giving and lifelong commitment, regardless of circumstances, is mandatory. Otherwise, the moment problems arise, mutual suspicion and dissatisfaction create mutual distrust, which then make Satan's temptation of extra-marital relationships ever more attractive.

Although the Bible does not forbid divorce altogether, it is limited only to instances whereby the other party has committed adultery or when an unbelieving spouse seeks separation due to religious differences. Other than these exceptions, divorce is prohibited. Our Lord Jesus said:

> *... What God has joined together, let man not separate.*
>
> **Matthew 19:6**

Personality conflicts and strained relationships do not constitute sufficient grounds for Christian couples to seek divorce. Both parties must try to win the other over with Christ's love through mutual acceptance, forgiveness and bearing with the weaknesses of the other.

The church must actively sound the alarm in opposition to social trends like homosexuality and domestic violence. Christians must realize that

> *Marriage should be honored by all, and the marriage bed kept pure, for God will judge the adulterer and all the sexually immoral.*
>
> **Hebrews 13:4**

We must also persuade those on the brink of sinful conduct to quickly repent and distance themselves from wicked ways, so that their lifestyles will be in keeping with biblical teaching and their status as Christians. The church must fill the gap in reviving familial values and rescuing Chinese society from moral bankruptcy and domestic decadence.

THE HOUSE CHURCH IN THE 21ST CENTURY

CHAPTER X

In 20 years of development, the house church of China has weathered much suffering. Under God's protection, she has sprouted roots, blossomed and borne abundant fruit. On this journey of growth filled with both successes and failures, she has had moments of brilliance as well as numerous blemishes. Facing the 21st Century, we in the Chinese house churches need to reassess and transform ourselves, affirming strengths and identifying weaknesses. Armed with lessons from the past, we will hopefully be able to better plan for the future in preparation to face even greater pressures and challenges. Based on our experiences and observations, the house churches possess the following strengths:

1. Biblically-Based Model: During Jesus' time, the Jews worshipped God in synagogues. Due to the serious decadence of religious scribes, priests and Pharisees, they possessed only an outward form of religiosity while living entirely contrary to God's will. Jesus led his disciples away from these religious meetings into Martha's house at Bethany (Matthew 21:12-17). The apostles placed even greater emphasis on house meetings, in the homes of Mark, Gaius, Priscilla and Aquila.

2. Convenience in Congregating: House churches facilitate easy gathering of neighbors as well as the evangelization of countless families. Be it in the villages or in the cities, the current political climate makes this the preferred church model for gathering, pastoring and managing the flock. Moreover, the elderly, the physically immobile and young children can easily be reached. Thus, every believer's home may be used by the Lord, and everyone has an opportunity to serve Him.

3. Flexibility and Adaptability: The Chinese house churches developed under unique circumstances: successive waves of political revolutions, expulsion of foreign missionaries, public humiliation of preachers, and demolition of church buildings. In particular, ten years of Cultural Revolution created a religious vacuum without pastors, Bibles or meeting places. Amidst such adverse conditions, God demonstrated His power through signs, wonders, miracles and spiritual gifts to draw people to faith in Christ. Christians huddled together secretly in homes under the protective cover of God's blessings. Ever ready to gather or disperse at a moment's notice, our strategy for ministry may be described as "guerilla-like."

4. Willingness to Pray: In the beginning, house church meetings were full of the elderly and the physically ill. Both preachers and Bibles were in scarce supply. These needy brothers and sisters would gather without any formal organization or structure. All they could do was fast and pray with tears rolling down their cheeks. Through prayer and fellowship, they understood God's will, and were comforted, healed and spiritually renewed. Everything was accomplished through prayer, which soon became an integral and wonderful part of the Chinese house church tradition.

5. Fervency in Evangelism: For 20 years, the house churches have actively responded to the mandate of the Great Commission by spreading the Gospel through relatives, friends and neighbors in all directions, near or far. The good news traversed from the villages into the cities, from the east to the west of the country, all the way into the midst of the minority tribespeople. Further, we have begun to participate in the larger vision of world evangelization.

6. Steadfastness in Truth and Exaltation of Christ: Preachers in China were driven by persecution to become part of the house churches because they insisted on biblical truth and maintained the supremacy of Jesus Christ. Emphasis is placed on Bible study, and in all things, they search the Bible for applicable principles. Their battle cry has been "Back to the Bible." Whenever contradictions with God's will occur, they would rather offend men than offend God, even to the extent of paying a heavy price for their religious commitments.

7. Separation of Church and State under the Lordship of Christ: The house churches constitute a spiritual bloc organizationally distinct from the TSPM. She is apolitical, unconnected to foreign authorities and unaffiliated with the denominations of old. The church is not characterized by political leanings, nor does she get entangled in political activities. However, her members are just as patriotic as any Chinese citizen, respecting and obeying all governing authorities. She is not controlled or manipulated by any foreign religious body, but does involve herself in complementary joint-ministries with overseas Christians and fellowship in the truth. These foreign Christians never become a part of the house churches. God's sovereignty over the Chinese house churches as exercised through the local leadership is always insisted upon.

8. Inherent Self-Government, Self-Sustenance and Self-Propagation: Although the house church did not participate in the Three-Self Patriotic Movement of the 1950s, she operated according to the Three-Self motto of self-governance, self-sustenance and self-propagation. None of her pastors was ordained by foreign religious groups, nor is she subject to the control of foreign entities. Under unique circumstances and the guidance of God, she birthed her own preachers and developed contextualized pastoral methods with missions strategies in accordance with national patriotism. Thus, the church keeps growing.

9. Strong Grassroots Ministries: The rapid expansion of the house churches is intimately intertwined with her network of tens of thousands of host families. Whether in the cities or in the villages, these families faithfully host God's servants and help them continue their itinerant ministries. Whenever a meeting came to a village, young and old would busily spread the word around, even bringing refreshments and stools to the host family where the meeting was to be held.

10. Leaders Called Directly by God: House church leaders are not appointed by government agencies. They are neither self-appointed nor did they get in through personal connections. On the contrary, they are spiritual leaders handpicked by God. With practical ministry experience, noble character and a spirit of self-sacrifice, they are blessed with spiritual gifts and wisdom from above. Through their hard work bearing much fruit, they earned the respect and adoration of brothers and sisters in Christ.

11. Ample Opportunity to Exercise Spiritual Gifts: House churches adopt the cell group format. Led by more mature members, everyone gathers for fellowship and interaction where one can freely share his or her feelings and ideas. Through ministry, petitionary prayer, blessings, worship, praise, exhortation and loving care, spiritual lives are built up and spiritual gifts are discovered and exercised.

12. Localized Worship and Ministry: Because house church preachers better understand individual needs, family situations and social issues, they can deliver messages which appropriately meet the immediate needs of their congregations. They possess neither profound theological theories nor eloquence of speech, yet they are able to satisfy spiritual needs. Based on the Bible and contextualized within local culture, they produce music, hymns, dramas and dance choreographies which are much loved by the brethren. As Paul wrote:

> *Let the word of Christ dwell in you richly as you teach and admonish one another with all wisdom, and as you sing psalms, hymns and spiritual songs with gratitude in your hearts to God.*
>
> ***Colossians 3:16***

13. Ability to Suffer and Bear One's Cross: The house churches belong to the underground church network that is unprotected by Chinese law. Preachers are often persecuted, where every meeting holds the possibility of arrest. Thus, without personal resolve to suffering and self-sacrifice, it is impossible for anyone to minister among the house churches. They live like fleeting shadows always on the run, possessing no permanent address, fame nor riches. Because they carry their own crosses, their messages are likewise focused on cross-bearing and following the Lord. Thus, the churches they lead are characterized by self-giving and sacrifice.

14. Abundant Full-Time Ministers: House church preachers do not receive a salary. Like the prophet Elijah, they rely by faith on God's provision. Those who willingly dedicate and devote their lives for the Lord are especially used by Him. They do not seek status, but only their Lord's pleasure, as they live a vagabond's life of itinerant traveling. The harvest we witness today in the Chinese house churches must be attributed to the thousands who continue to selflessly give of themselves.

15. Better Ministerial Unity among Co-Workers: Most evangelists found their mission fields because of persecution that forced them to leave their hometowns. Dedicated to one another, they complement and serve together, drawing on each other's strengths and overcoming weaknesses. In full devotion to God, the mission and the co-workers, they nurture a spirit of team ministry. With common vision, resolution and language, they are able to pursue a common goal and produce results. Much like the church at Philippi, their "partnership in the gospel from the first day until now" is praiseworthy (Philippians 1:5).

16. Sensitive Discernment and Effective Repulsion of Heresies: Although house church preachers lack formal theological training, they are especially sensitive where heresies are concerned. While on the one hand they evangelize unbelievers and establish churches, they instruct the brethren in polemics on the other. With a relatively better grasp of the local church situation where congregation sizes are small and easily manageable, these preachers emphasize Bible study and are able to effectively understand each person's background, beliefs and motivations. Thus, we have gradually developed an effective strategy on countering heresy.

17. Innovative Ministry through the Spirit: The house churches are characterized by loose organization which is democratic and free from clergy control, rules and regulations. Ministry is carried out in absolute dependence upon the Holy Spirit's guidance rather than experience. Believers pray earnestly and thirst for the Spirit's filling, thus creating a spiritual atmosphere in the church where the Spirit is actively at work. We firmly believe:

> *"Not by might nor by power, but by my Spirit," says the Lord Almighty.*
>
> ***Zechariah 4:6***

18. Establishment upon the Body of Christ: The Lord Jesus said:

> *... on this rock I will build my church, and the gates of Hades will not overcome it.*
>
> ***Matthew 16:18***

The faith of the house churches is founded upon these very words. She will neither follow worldly trends nor be fickle under changing circumstances, but will stand firm on God's promises through all adversity. Like a house that has its foundation on the rock, the house churches will never collapse (See Matthew 7:24-27).

19. Increased Connectivity with Affiliated Churches: For 20 years, house church preachers have been preoccupied with their itinerant evangelism ministries through which they established the churches they currently lead. Over time, mutually exclusive cliques have been formed that even rebuke and attack one another. As the spiritual body of Christ grows in stature, it has come to understand the naivete and sinfulness of such conduct. Co-workers in affiliated churches agreed to lay down personal prejudices as we harvest together in mutual cordiality and acceptance. Through this, bridges to unity have been built.

20. No Extra-Ecclesial Restrictions: In some respect, one may say that the house churches are "unfreely free" and "disobediently obedient." She takes direct instruction from and obeys her Lord Jesus Christ, and will never subject herself to manipulation from any other source. This is precisely the reason why she has been persecuted. Although house church Christians live in an environment where their freedom is curbed, yet in their hearts they are truly free. Despite refusing to be subject to the many regulative straitjackets with which the earthly government has tried to restrain their religious freedom, believers submit themselves to all social policies and systems that do not conflict with their Christian faith.

21. Source of Calming Influence in Society: Even though the house churches are neither formally recognized nor legally protected by the government and constantly misunderstood and misrepresented by the authorities, in reality they play an indubitable role in public security and welfare. Christianity emphasizes the following: filial piety, marital love, parental guidance, cordial neighborliness, honoring authorities, obeying laws, curbing crime, doing good, seeking peace, opposing violence, rejecting, promiscuity, etc. House church believers discipline themselves to

> *Live a life worthy of the calling you have received.*
> ***Ephesians 4:1***

22. Emphasis on Mutuality and Reflection: The house church is not a self-enclosed entity privately concocting her own brew but, rather, she blends herself into the larger global family of Christians. The true house church is intimately intertwined with historically orthodox theology. She understands history, is aware of the times, and is steadfast on orthodox beliefs. In ministry, she is constantly *"transformed by the renewing of [her] mind"* (Romans 12:2) through critical reflection, self-awareness, complementing with affiliated churches in balancing out strengths and weaknesses, and actual experience itself.

23. Emphasis on Christian Education of Youth: Young people constitute the future hope of both the nation as well as the church. We recognize the importance of their education and have organized numerous short training sessions that help establish their faith beliefs and nurture their spiritual lives. Once they enter the secular world, our hope is that the training they have received will guard them from sinful influences and temptations: adultery, drugs, fighting, deceit, deception, and even getting mesmerized by cults both here and abroad.

24. Vision for World Missions: The house churches have a slogan: "Bring the gospel back to Jerusalem." They have big hearts driven by indebtedness. Realizing that Western missionaries weathered many dangers in order to bring the good news to them, they now feel that they have an obligation to pass the Gospel on to others in need. For this reason, many of our young people right now are learning English and some are learning Arabic. Their studies include local culture, customs and habits, so that they may become better equipped as useful instruments in the hands of God.

25. Preparations for World Missions Involvement: Since Robert Morrison of the London Missionary Society entered China, Protestantism has been in China for almost 200 years. These 200 years of history have been marked by blood, sweat and tears. Countless missionaries left behind their loved ones and dedicated their lives by coming to this backward and impoverished piece of foreign land. Here, they started their lifetime of evangelization. Yet, their love for Chinese souls was not reciprocated by a warm Chinese welcome. On the contrary, they were viewed as enemies, possibly due to the Chinese ego, blind anti-foreign sentiments or express anger against Western powers. Such wrath found its victim in the missionary. During those years, there were instances of anti-religious riots all over the country. Many church buildings were damaged. Worthy of special mention is the Boxer Rebellion of 1900, when, under the instigation and manipulation of the Empress Dowager Cixi, the rebels directed their fury by unleashing a massacre on meek and mild missionaries. Numerous missionaries lost their lives, and many families were exterminated.

Missionary contributions to China in the fields of medicine, education and philanthropy were significant. Even more so, they brought the invaluable message of the good news. Their dedication went unappreciated by the Chinese people and eventually they were even branded as "imperialist lackeys." After 1949, missionaries were ruthlessly expelled from China. Although they could not move the Chinese church toward revival, these missionaries had already sowed the seeds of the Gospel on Chinese soil. Through the zeniths and nadirs of the tumultuous years that followed, the Chinese church withstood wave upon wave of attacks. In particular, the Cultural Revolution that sought to eradicate all forms of religion and superstition mercilessly persecuted Christians. Yet, not only did the church in China survive eradication, the house church started taking baby steps on the road to maturity as she gradually gained strength. As of this day, the Gospel has taken root, blossomed and borne fruit on Chinese soil. Not only have God's children not been silenced, they have grown up into the vibrant house churches of China that have gained the world's attention.

House churches from all over China have responded to the Great Commission by fanning the fires of unprecedented missionary fervor. Today, she is taking on a larger burden and shouldering a greater responsibility as she prepares to enter the harvest fields of world evangelization. This is no longer a pipe dream, but a slogan and it is moving toward an actual missionary movement. God has placed the Chinese church in the midst of suffering and trial. This must somehow be part of His wonderful purpose.

From the perspective of church history, whenever God chooses to use the church from a particular nation, that church must possess the following precedents and prerequisites:

1. The church must have experienced great revival
2. She must have withstood tremendous suffering and trial
3. Many young people are raised from among her ranks
4. Her members have had experience in active evangelism
5. They have a vision for world missions
6. They have ever increasing educational levels
7. Their country is riding the crest of an economic boom

8. They are constantly reforming toward globalization

The church in China has all these credentials. She has taken shape, and this should be the time for her to prepare for action. China's next harvest field ought to include the Arab world. This is a hard and tough piece of land to till. All the financial resources of the churches in Western nations will not accomplish this task. Only Jesus Christ's love can transform hearts and dissolve enmity.

26. Attention-Grabbing by Sheer Numbers: The size of the Chinese house church is staggering, a fact recognized by observers both local and foreign. During the Cultural Revolution, Mao Zedong's wife Jiang Qing once proclaimed: "Let the Christians go meet the devil in hell! The Bible will only be found in museums." Little did she know that when she died, tens of thousands of churches all over the country were being established. There are reportedly no less than 80 million Christians in the house church today. This is proof that God is blessing China.

Although the house churches have been graciously blessed by God and possess many strengths, there are negative aspects with regard to her current situation and present condition. For instance:

I. Lack of Holistic and Systematic Theological Training: For various reasons, most house churches emphasize widespread evangelism to the neglect of theological training. Thus, the church has lost her balance, sometimes resulting in confusion, erroneous interpretations of Scripture and even the spawn of extremist and heretical cults. As an adaptive measure to meet the church's developmental needs, we have doubled up our efforts at organizing a variety of theological classes that will nurture more talent for the church.

II. Preachers Lacking Formal Education: Right now, few preachers in China possess high academic credentials. Most of them hail from villages where their parishioners are relatively less cultured and this has affected the overall quality of the house churches. To attempt to change this phenomenon is no easy task because the cultural level of believers is tied to national standards for education. Thus, this will be a long and arduous process that needs constant encouragement from parents with regard to their children's education. It also requires that young people recognize the crisis they are in and become active learners who develop good learning habits. The church has to organize classes on literacy, English and computer skills. We will make every effort to facilitate their future enrollment in universities and colleges.

III. Difficulties in Pastoral Follow-Up: In the 1980s and 90s, the house churches experienced an unprecedented great revival. People flooded the churches in search of biblical truth. Yet, this wonderful phenomenon has also put overwhelming pressure on preachers since each person must pastor so many parishioners. As a result, many congregations are left without a shepherd. Such churches are unhealthy, weak and often stray from orthodoxy. Moreover, the preachers themselves are of lesser culture and have had no theological training as they minister to farmer believers in tentmaking fashion. More manpower, material and financial resources will help strengthen our training and nurturing of co-workers that satisfy the church's growing needs.

IV. Less Than Ideal Church Management: Due to a lack of hierarchical structure, there are many loopholes within house church organizations. Thus, they often find themselves caught between two dilemmas: either an impractical overemphasis on structure in a bid to protect the church from secularization and mechanization, which our political climate does not allow; or a disorganized and loose association, which leads to confusion, disorderliness, lack of a centripetal unifying force and ultimately to the demise of ministry itself. Moreover, poor church management provides inroads for heresies and cults to infiltrate church ranks. We need to ask God for divine blessings of wisdom so we may know how to be better stewards in this regard.

V. Ecclesial Sectarianism and Exclusivism: There are many reasons for the disarray among house churches, including geographical spread, narrowness of leaders, scarcity of interaction, diverse theological insights, and lack of understanding and knowledge of true unity. Such sectarianism has deprived the church as a whole of bearing collective testimony to Christ's glory. The Lord's name is shamed when those opposed to Him use ecclesial disunity and fragmentation as a launch pad for attacks. May the Lord have mercy upon the house churches of China and remove the barriers which church groups have set up to seclude themselves and exclude others. May His church be soon unified in the truth!

VI. Passive Tendency toward the World: The house churches grew amidst persecution. Believers were not granted freedom to gather and preachers had no freedom to teach as the house churches lost all autonomy to speak or act. Prolonged exposure to such oppressive regulations has caused the church to become passive and pessimistic with respect to the world. Such attitudes have taken shape over a long process. If the government were to gradually adopt a more open attitude, I think these tendencies in the church would also ultimately change.

VII. Easily Misunderstood by the Government: Since the government has refused to recognize the house churches as a legitimate religious entity, oppression is commonplace. Believers have had to resort to clandestine meetings as a way of getting around the system. In the event that they get arrested, the Public Security Bureau never fails to put them through intense interrogation. What house church brothers and sisters fear most is implicating other brethren on their account. Thus, staying silent is the usual strategy of choice. Unfortunately, the government has thereby grown a sense of suspicion toward house church Christians since they often meet at night and passively oppose the government. Christians could possibly harbor subversive intentions that threaten the government's existence.

VIII. Deprived of Public Meeting Places: Due to the limited floor area of host family homes, we are forced to put a cap on the number of attendees. Should we have too many participants, we will distribute the brethren to separate homes, a situation which then creates a need for even more pastoral workers to manage the flock. With the house churches already facing a lack of pastors, this inability to hold larger meetings has become our greatest problem. If the government were willing to allow the house churches to meet openly in their own buildings for nurturing workers and regular gatherings, then the church would be able to develop in a healthy manner.

IX. Easily Attacked by Cults: Without legal protection from government authorities, the house churches have become favorite targets of cultists, since house church believers and preachers themselves are targeted by the government. The Eastern Lightning Cult has taken advantage of this lack of security to attack and kidnap house church Christians, who do not dare report such harassment out of fear for their own safety. The Public Security Bureau often ends up pursuing them instead of the Eastern Lightning cultists.

X. Denial of Positive Social Image: The Chinese people label Christianity as a Western religion, missionaries as "foreign devils," and Chinese believers as "pseudo-foreign devils." Christianity is considered "the opium of the people" or "a lackey of imperialism." Thus, Christians have become second-class citizens, often existing like dogs with tails between their legs. Good deeds of love performed by Christians do not receive formal recognition. It is extremely difficult for Christian virtue, character, conduct and social influence to be considered positively by the Chinese government.

XI. Poverty and Instability of the Preacher's Life: House church preachers have chosen a path marked by self-sacrifice, suffering and cross-bearing. Over all these years, countless in their vocation have been imprisoned and fined, driving them to the point of severe poverty, where their houses are in shambles and their children have no money for proper food or clothing, let alone to be able to go school. With possible persecution always around the next corner, families of preachers often live with fear and trepidation. They live a life with neither a firm foundation nor a safe haven. Every Christian's prayer before God is for religious freedom to quickly dawn on China, so that everyone can lead normal lives.

XII. Shortage of Funds and Subjectivity to Temptation or Control: Since most house churches are found in the farming communities, their lifestyles are further down the poverty spectrum. Thus, preachers hardly speak on financial contribution. Yet, there are massive budgets to be met for ministry expenses like missions, itinerant pastoring, administration, co-worker training, theological education, and emergency funds, which need the contribution and cooperation of each and every brother and sister in Christ. Foreign financial aid has often resulted in a dilemma of either temptation for the receiver or control by the giver through overdependence. Church co-workers find themselves in a complicated, no-win situation with no idea of a good way out. It is reasonable to expect a church's resources to come from the contributions of its own members. Where circumstances allow for it, tentmaking ministers must be encouraged to develop economic opportunities for generating funds. Through various means and ministries, the church must pursue the ultimate goal of financial independence and self-sustenance.

If house church leaders are able to constantly reflect, evaluate, contextualize, renew and project their visions for ministry, then the house church will always be evergreen, perpetually youthful, healthy and growing.

CONCLUSION

by Dr. David Hunt
President, WorldServe Ministries

Well, the story of Brother Shen is now out. You may have some questions on your mind. What will happen to him? Will he have to go into hiding once again? Will he be arrested? Will his ministry be curtailed?

Perhaps all of these things and more will happen. Knowing this, you may be asking why he has chosen to go public at all—and why now.

This isn't a man writing his memoirs long after the action is finished. Brother Shen is the current, active leader of China Gospel Fellowship, one of the largest of China's house church movements. Every year they establish hundreds of new churches with tens of thousands of new believers.

So why go public? Why now?

I have asked those same questions and many more. In fact, I have really struggled over this and I have been concerned enough that I delayed the publishing of this book for some time. I am still concerned but Brother Shen and our team have carefully and prayerfully weighed the cost.

Let me explain the why this way. After Brother Shen was kidnapped by Eastern Lightning, China Gospel Fellowship was reeling from this terribly traumatic ordeal. The families of all 34 who were kidnapped were shaken and concerned for their loved ones. We were in touch with Brother Shen and asked if he would like to meet with us to explore how we could help the families and China Gospel Fellowship.

He went to his wife and explained that some people he had not yet met face-to-face wanted to meet him to explore ways to help. His wife was alarmed. He had just been released from a cult after going to a meeting that he thought was with some Christian foreigners. How could he even consider doing this?

He took another great step of faith and came to the

meeting. He entered the room and greeted us, then right away asked if we would mind if he made a phone call. He called his wife to tell her he had arrived safely and was not in danger from these foreigners. He then told us about the significance of the meeting for him, his wife and China Gospel Fellowship.

He told us about the terrible ordeal of being kidnapped and held forcibly by the Eastern Lightning cult. He related to us how his family and all the others had suffered and he explained how it had sent shock waves through China Gospel Fellowship. He told us that he was compelled to come and share with his brothers and sisters in Christ because the burden was too great for him to bear. He wanted the truth to be known and he wanted our understanding and he was hoping we could help tangibly.

As he concluded, he boldly told us it was now our burden to bear, as well. I spoke on behalf of those gathered and told him that we accepted the burden and the responsibility and that we would help.

Why is Brother Shen going public now? He is a very principled man and it greatly bothers him that there is so much misunderstanding about the underground church. He feels it is time to share the truth about the situation in China relating to religious freedom, and his prayer is that the church in the West will understand, pray, stand with them and help in a tangible way. I too feel that it is time to share the burden of responsibility with the rest of the Body of Christ. The Church in China is suffering, it is in need, and we have a biblical and moral responsibility to stand with them and help them. It is wrong for us to do anything less. James, inspired by the Holy Sprit, wrote,

> *Anyone, then, who knows the good he ought to do and doesn't do it, sins.*
>
> ***James 4:17***

As I have had the privilege to meet many other leaders of other house church movements, I can assure you that Brother Shen is not only sharing a perspective from China Gospel Fellowship, he is sharing what is on the heart of every leader of every house church group in China today. They want the world to know the truth about the situation in China but they especially want their brothers and sisters outside China to know the truth.

They are unanimous in the declaration that there is no religious freedom in China today.

I have been with Chinese leaders of the underground church when they address this most painful of topics for them. I have seen them weep because of the hurt that brothers and sisters outside have caused. They tell us they can take the beatings, the persecution, the confiscation of their property, and the imprisonment, but there are two things they struggle with the most:

- not being able to care for their families, especially while incarcerated or in hiding, and
- the lies believed by the Body of Christ about the situation in China today

Although the Church in China is suffering and in great need, they are victorious and joyful! They don't live with self-pity or with a defeatist outlook. They walk the way of the cross with deep joy and great confidence, standing for Christ in the face of great adversity.

The underground Church in China is not political and they wish the Chinese government would not be threatened by them, but instead, understand they are the best of citizens. However, despite the risks, the house churches will continue to meet together, and proclaim the Gospel of Jesus Christ, whether it is permitted or not. Without the ability to meet together in worship and proclaim the Gospel, how can there be the religious freedom the government claims?

They want you, the body of Christ outside China, to know they love you and pray for you. They want you to know that although there is not religious freedom, they are committed to serving Jesus Christ as Lord. If that means they must go to prison, they do so bravely and honorably. They call prison a time of rest and higher education, when in fact they are beaten, often daily, and forced to do hard labor 16 hours a day. They tell us they can bear that because of what Christ has done for them.

What they have great difficulty bearing is the lie being perpetuated by many that this is not taking place. It is like pouring salt in their wounds when they hear the statements of well-known Christian leaders from the West talking about how they should register with the government. They are appalled at the lack of understanding. The house church leaders find it incomprehensible that churches in the West pour millions of dollars into the Three-Self Patriotic Movement, a government organization established to control the church. They declare that Jesus Christ is the head of the Church, not the communist party.

Our brothers and sisters in Christ in the Underground Church in China have been hurt deeply by the lack of understanding. They simply want the truth known. They want to share with you their great victories, and they desire fellowship with the body of Christ.

These precious servants never ask us for anything so I will ask for them.

I phrase it in the context of James 4:17, *when we know the good we ought to do and don't do it, it is sin.* We have a biblical responsibility to help our suffering brothers and sisters. We—the Church, the Body of Christ—have the means to provide for every family suffering because of a loved one in prison for his or her faith.

We have the ability to help replace the possessions that are routinely confiscated. We have the ability to provide the Bibles they all deeply covet.

We have the ability to provide a subsistence level of support for the church planters, as they want to serve the Lord full-time but struggle because they are so poor. They are giving their families, their lives, their health, their all, to serve the Lord. We can't do what they are doing in bringing the Gospel to every village and city in China, but we can enable and equip them to go.

My prayer is that we, the body of Christ outside China, provide for the greatest concerted outreach the nation of China has ever seen and mobilize 10,000 church planters to reach this nation for Christ. This can be done! The servants of God are in place and they are willing to take up their cross. Are you willing to walk with them?

I trust that you have been encouraged by the story of Brother Shen. May the faith and strength of our Chinese brothers and sisters in Christ encourage you with whatever challenges you may be facing. Regardless of circumstances, we too can be victorious, joyful and immersed in the peace of God that passes all understanding, because He has promised, "Never will I leave you or forsake you."

I welcome you to our website at www.worldserve.org to find out how you can join hands with our brothers and sisters in China and elsewhere. You can be the one to stand with them, encourage them and help them. You can make a difference in China today! On behalf of our brothers and sisters in Christ in China, I thank you for whatever the Lord puts on your heart.

Dr. David Hunt, President WorldServe Ministries

Please go to www.worldserve.org
to find out how you can help